A WORLD OF INSECURITY

A WORLD OF
INSECURITY

DEMOCRATIC DISENCHANTMENT
IN RICH AND POOR COUNTRIES

PRANAB BARDHAN

HARVARD UNIVERSITY PRESS

CAMBRIDGE, MASSACHUSETTS & LONDON, ENGLAND

2022

First printing

Cataloging-in-Publication Data is available from the Library of Congress.
ISBN: 9780674259843 (alk. paper)

Contents

A WORLD OF INSECURITY

Introduction

In 1938, shortly before his exile from Nazi Germany, the writer Thomas Mann warned an American audience that democracy "should put aside the habit of taking itself for granted, of self-forgetfulness." In recent years liberals in many democracies have been rudely jolted out of their it-can't-happen-here complacency. Late on election night, November 8, 2016, Paul Krugman wrote about Donald Trump in the *New York Times,* "people like me, and probably like most readers of The New York Times, truly didn't understand the country we live in. We thought that our fellow citizens would not, in the end, vote for a candidate . . . so scary yet ludicrous" (Krugman 2016). About two and half years before that night, many liberals in India felt something similar at Narendra Modi's massive victory—though, one should say, Modi is scary but not ludicrous.

The challenge to liberal democracy, occasionally from the Left but mostly from right-wing demagogues, is worldwide. Let us cite some global statistics. In 2021, the V-Dem Institute at the University of Gothenburg, Sweden, produced the largest global data set on democracy, covering about two hundred countries, measuring democracy in disaggregated, multidimensional ways, involving over thirty-five hundred scholars and experts. The institute's report is grim reading:

- Autocracies now rule the majority of people—in eighty-seven countries that are home to 68 percent of the global population.
- Liberal democracies diminished over the past decade, from forty-one countries to thirty-two, and now have a population share of only 14 percent.
- About one-third of the world's people—that is, 2.6 billion people—live in nations undergoing "autocratization"; only 4 percent live under regimes that are becoming more democratic.
- Autocratization has affected major countries like Brazil, India, Poland, Turkey, and the United States.
- Latin America is back to a level of democracy last recorded in the early 1990s, while Eastern Europe and Central Asia are at post–Soviet Union lows.
- India, with its population of nearly 1.4 billion, used to be the world's largest democracy; it is now described as an electoral autocracy due to the severe shrinking of space for the media, civil society, and political opposition under the current government.
- Attacks on freedom of expression and the right to peaceful assembly and protest, and assaults on the media and academic and other civil society institutions, are intensifying across the world; the quality of elections is deteriorating.

Other outlets measuring democracy in the world—like the American Enterprise Institute, the Economist Intelligence Unit, Freedom House, and the Polity data series—report similar trends.

Such attacks have often been carried out in democracies in recent years by elected leaders and politicians. In fact, as Steven Levitsky and Daniel Ziblatt show in *How Democracies Die* (2018), in the last three decades democratic breakdowns have been caused less often by military generals and soldiers in coups or other violent seizures of power than by elected governments themselves. While citizens are under the spell of some "strong" leader's heroic antics and seductive promises, democratic institutions and buffers and associated civic norms gradually erode until one day, as in the case of the fabled frog slowly boiled to death, democracy ends not with a bang but a whimper. As Levitsky and Ziblatt point out, "The tragic paradox of the electoral route to authoritarianism is that democracy's assassins use the very institutions of democracy—gradually, subtly, and even legally—to kill it." This has been all too familiar to liberal citizens in Hungary, India, Russia, and Turkey in recent years under elected strong leaders like Viktor Orbán, Narendra Modi, Vladimir Putin, and Recep Tayyip Erdoğan, respectively. The United States had a narrow escape in 2021, thanks largely to its battered but still (partially) resilient institutions, but many remain doubtful for the future and do not rule out the rise of another leader, possibly less ludicrous than Trump but at least as scary.

In reaction to these unfolding challenges to liberal democracy there has been a burgeoning of both popular and academic literature that seeks to understand their origins, history, and patterns and what to do about them. This book belongs to that general category, but it is different in some major ways. First, while most of the literature concerns Europe and the United States, this analysis combines the perspectives of rich industrial countries and relatively poor developing countries, emphasizing similarities and differences in problems and antidotes alike.

Second, while many have pointed to the large rise in inequality in the past few decades, this book will give at least equal attention to the distinctive problems of *insecurity,* both economic and cultural, and the diverse forms they take in various countries. Apart from pointing to the usual political-economy factors, this may lend a bit of global and cultural sensibility to a study of democracy's vulnerabilities. One hopes that this may lead to a more nuanced and broad-based understanding of a present and looming menace on our democratic horizon in different parts of the world. As the author is a long-term resident academic in the United States and a lifelong researcher on India's political economy and culture, the reader may expect that the book will give particular attention to the dysfunctionalities of these two largest democracies.

Marking a third difference from much of the literature, this book will also assess the alternative model of authoritarian capitalism, which the Chinese success story has showcased in recent years. It will discuss the negative features of that model even from the point of view of development, not to speak of the intrinsic value of democratic freedom and autonomy. It will also show how some of the undeniable strengths of the Chinese governance system and state capacity are not necessarily due to its authoritarianism but more to certain distinctive features of its historical legacy.

Finally, this book will also propose a superior organizational alternative. Specifically, it will recommend a rejuvenation of social democracy, with some necessary modifications in systems of capitalist innovation and governance, along with a restructuring of capital-labor relations and redistributive public finance.

In recent writings there has been an understandable preoccupation with the immediate problems of recovery from the COVID-19 pandemic, the economic collapse in its wake, and the mountains of debt left for economies to tackle.

During the pandemic many social commentators in the claustrophobic gloom of their self-isolation have written in somewhat feverish, apocalyptic terms about the near future. Some expect the preexisting dysfunctionalities of social and political institutions to accelerate in a postpandemic world, anticipating a plunge into a vicious spiral.

Others are more hopeful, envisaging a world where people wake up to the deep fault lines the coronavirus crisis has revealed and try to build a better world.

A number of commentators have turned to literary narratives of pestilence of one form or another to make sense of the crisis, referring to Albert Camus's *The Plague* in the Algerian city of Oran; Eugène Ionesco's *Rhinoceros,* in which a strange disease turns humans into rhinoceroses in a small French village; José Saramago's *Blindness* and its portrayal of a mass epidemic of blindness in an unnamed city with a heavy-handed government; and the more recent *Book of M* by Peng Shepherd, where the infected find that they cast no shadow and soon lose their memory. These works are rich and complex enough to feed both fears and hopes. All are narratives of human frailty and social breakdown, but also of human resilience, as in the portrayal of the respective doctors in the novels of Camus and Saramago. (The narratives of Camus and Ionesco have also been interpreted as analogies for the reactions of ordinary people to the creeping fascism of occupied France.)

This book, like the aforementioned narratives, takes both anxieties and aspirations seriously, adopting what might be called an upbeat skepticism: pushing for things to get better while being aware that they may not, somewhat akin to what Antonio Gramsci (2011) called "pessimism of the intellect, optimism of the will." But it also tries to put the pandemic in perspective. Without ignoring the scarring effects of the pandemic, it pays more attention to the long-term systemic issues that face democracies.

The pandemic was, of course, only one of many things that heightened our anxieties in this age of insecurity. Over the last two decades the world has been subject to many traumatic events—international terrorism, civil wars with all their destruction and exodus of refugees, the financial crisis of 2007–2009, the debt and currency crises (particularly in Europe and Latin America), stringent and wrenching austerity policies, deep slumps in many economies, large-scale job losses, technological disruptions, creeping authoritarianism and ethnonationalist excesses, the increasing incidence of natural disasters (probably attributable to ongoing climate change), agro-ecological distress, mass dislocations, and a series of epidemics (COVID-19 being the latest). All of this has dangerously exposed the fragility and insecurity of the lives and livelihoods of billions of ordinary people. This has been particularly acute in developing countries, where numerous people live a hand-to-mouth existence even in the best of times, with very little in the form of social insurance or feasible alternative ways or places to live. Recently a research team offered a way of tracking global economic and policy uncertainty simply by counting the occurrence of that term in the country reports produced for 143 nations by the Economist Intelligence Unit. While their World Uncertainty Index is obviously a crude measure, it shows strikingly that, by the end of the 2020s, the incidence of "uncertainty" was about 50 percent higher than it had been in years 1996 to 2010.

The real import of the pandemic may be less as a discrete event than as a force multiplier, making all these problems worse. Long before the pandemic, the protective guardrails of liberal democracies were already under severe stress; of course, under the cover of the pandemic, and in the name of disease surveillance and quarantine, demagogic populists have done yet more damage to democratic institutions and expressions of protest. Similarly, the great variance among countries rich and poor in their damage control efforts and the rates of recovery and of vaccination and other prophylactic measures cannot but have a continuing impact on political structures. And now with Putin's invasion of Ukraine, global geopolitical and economic uncertainties have been raised a few more notches.

This book looks at the impact of large-scale uncertainty and insecurity on political-economic structures, including the democratic state, various social coordination mechanisms, and their ideological underpinnings at both the local community and the general macrolevel, and explores some policy options for this age of insecurity, using the lens of both rich and poor countries.

Here is a brief outline of the subsequent chapters. Chapter 1 discusses the populist challenges to the liberal order, tracing their roots less to inequality and more to insecurity—not only economic insecurity of incomes and jobs but also cultural insecurity, the latter varying between rich and poor countries though similar in some other respects. There is popular resentment against the professional and cultural elite in both sets of countries, more than against the financial elite. The so-called culture wars often favor right-wing populists over the Left. Immigration has been a major cultural issue in Europe and the United States, while religious fanaticism has been important in Brazil, India, and Turkey. The chapter ends with a discussion of the toxic role of social media in sharpening polarization and spewing ethnic vitriol.

Among recent populist demands there have been vociferous calls for "taking back control" from distant politicians and officials. Chapter 2 discusses the case for restoring autonomy and control to the local community level. In view of egregious state and market failures, there has been a tendency even among some liberals now to turn to local community, utilizing its advantages in local information, relations of trust and reciprocity, and public participation in bottom-up decision-making in solving local problems. But there are also some striking community failures that should make us wary of the various political and economic pitfalls of the communitarian position.

The other demand for taking back control has involved the political community that takes the form of a nation-state, rejecting the ideas of cosmopolitan liberals and the restrictions imposed by irksome international rules and agreements. Chapter 3 discusses how the resurgent nationalism all around the world today is one of narrow, divisive, tribalist ethnonationalism. As an alternative, it points to the more inclusive idea of civic nationalism that has been particularly prominent in the histories of two large, diverse democracies, India and the United States, since independence (until recently). Ethnic nationalism rides roughshod over this diversity, and is suspicious of dissident groups and minorities as possible fifth columnists. Civic nationalism, however, has some fragility and often provides too thin a basis for political mobilization. The economic consequences of the policies flowing from these two alternative kinds of nationalism are discussed.

As an alternative to the tiresome procedures of liberal democracy, some populists hanker after a strong leader and state. Chapter 4 discusses the allure of authoritarian capitalism that the formidable success of the China model has brought to the foreground in both rich and poor countries. After a general discussion of the prerequisites of a strong state and the ingredients of state capacity, the chapter delves into the Chinese governance system, taking the discussion beyond the standard and simplistic trope of democracy versus authoritarianism. It shows that some of the positive features of Chinese governance (like career incentives for officials to promote local development, and decentralizing the structure of management of infrastructure building and local business development) do not necessarily depend on the authoritarian system; some variants of them can very well be adopted, with proper reforms of organization and incentives, in a democratic country. Even for the remarkable general ability of the Chinese top leadership to quickly coordinate and mobilize the state machinery, authoritarianism is neither necessary nor sufficient. The chapter also explores how some of the major problems in Chinese governance arise from its lack of downward accountability; its choking of information flows, delaying course correction in case of serious mistakes in decisions; its lack of public scrutiny of corrupt collusion between officials and businessmen; and its systemic tendency in the face of a crisis to overreact, suppress information, and act heavy-handedly, thereby making the system less resilient. These are all ugly features of authoritarianism that one should seriously take into account, even if one cares mainly about growth performance of a system and not the intrinsic value of democratic freedom.

Even in countries that are not directly responding to the siren song of authoritarianism and do place some value on contested elections, there is now a tendency for democracies to be hollowed out by a crude form of majoritarianism that endangers the civil rights of minorities but is quite attractive to populists from majority ethnic groups (such as Catholic nationalists in Poland, Hindu nationalists in India, Islamists in Indonesia and Turkey, and white evangelicals in Brazil and the United States). Chapter 5 discusses what happens when minorities lack both the numerical strength and the financial clout to withstand the majoritarian onslaught. Separation of powers and other constitutional checks and balances are the traditional, still important, safeguards for democracy in such cases, along with vigorous media, universities, and other civil society institutions. In some contexts social diversity and fragmentation may allow for tactical alliances to protect minorities, and for preservation of an implicit social contract in which the minimum civil rights of all groups are more or less assured.

Chapter 6 explores the possibility of rejuvenating social democracy as a feasible alternative, albeit with substantial modifications to its older forms. In some detail, it explores the general idea of social democracy as constituting a kind of ideological balance between different foundational values and between the alternative social coordination mechanisms a society might use to act according to its values. The chapter then analyzes the reasons for the decline of social democratic parties in recent decades, and examines ways of reviving the salience of the idea of social democracy under the constraints and opportunities of the pandemic-marred world. It argues that, in a world of heightened inequality and insecurity and with the prevailing acceptance of a more assertive role of the state, social democrats can promote a more active restructuring of welfare policies. But—also at the community level—social democratic labor and civil society organizations must provide leadership that counters race-to-the bottom community and nationalist pursuits and must recapture the local cultural territory appropriated by the populists. To do so, social democrats have to be more sensitive to the genuine communitarian needs and the cultural neglect that workers feel in their relation to the more cosmopolitan, liberal.

Chapter 7 examines the fraught relationship between social democracy and capitalism and discusses ways of restructuring it to the benefit of all stakeholders—capital, labor, and the community of involved citizens. It argues for a set of modifications in capitalist governance that, while they must not interfere with firms' innovative capacities, may actually encourage a change in the pattern of innovations in a socially beneficial direction. Also discussed are needs for significant reforms in the financial system, labor market policy, and election funding for a social democracy to function properly.

Under the general rubric of social democracy Chapters 8 and 9 consider a limited number of specific policies to relieve the surging insecurity in the world. Chapter 8 assesses the desirability and feasibility of a universal basic income as part of a citizen's right to minimum economic security. Such minimum economic security is often almost totally absent in poor countries, particularly in their large informal sectors. Many consider the costs of a universal basic income prohibitively high in rich countries, but in poor countries the costs may be somewhat more manageable. Chapter 8 suggests, after scrutiny of different kinds of financial resources and various implementation issues, that a universal basic income supplement at a decent level may not be unaffordable in a lower-middle-income country like India.

Chapter 9 considers a number of other policies to relieve the mounting problems of economic and cultural insecurity afflicting lives all around. It first addresses the problem of job security and suggests various ways of creating good jobs, particularly those that are also consistent with environmental goals. It then calls for reshaping the pattern and direction of public research to serve the goal of improving the life of common people, including the expansion of job prospects. It goes into governance issues, first on the advantages and disadvantages of decentralization, and second on ways of mitigating the pervasive scourge of corruption that erodes trust in democracy, particularly in developing countries. International coordination through institutions and agreements will, it argues, be imperative to harmonize policies and prevent a race to the bottom. Finally, the chapter describes how labor organizations can be mobilized to step into the cultural void in the lives of working people— a void that currently is being filled by the false bravado and venomous conspiracy theories of populist leaders.

One running theme of the chapters is that there are no easy solutions to many of the problems for democracy that have been identified, and even in the narrow pathways of some discernible solutions there are pitfalls at every step that we have to be wary of. Yet there is hope that social democracy, which has gone through rough patches in recent decades, can be revived with some adjustments, compromises, and innovations to serve at least as a dependable lighthouse amid the dark and choppy waters of our world of insecurity.

1

Insecurity, Inequality, and Democracy

In the last four decades, world democracy has seen some dramatic changes. In the 1980s democracy was restored to Brazil with a landmark constitution, after two decades of military rule. In the early 1990s came the historic end of the autocratic regimes of the Soviet Union and its allies in eastern Europe, soon followed by another historic end, that of the apartheid regime in South Africa (and of the regime of Augusto Pinochet in Chile somewhat earlier). In the late 1990s democracy was restored in Indonesia (after many decades of military rule) and Nigeria (after military rule off and on in previous decades). In the three decades up to 2010 the world's largest democracy, India, saw a remarkable widening of its democratic empowerment of hitherto subordinate social groups and castes (which some have described as tantamount to a social revolution).

Along with these positive developments the last four decades have also seen some broad economic and political changes that have ended up shrinking the horizon of democracy. These decades have seen a rise of finance capital in much of the capitalist world (widening the gulf between Wall Street and Main Street), with its excesses causing not just the worldwide financial crisis of 2007–2009 but a general public distrust in economic and political institutions that form the basic foundations of democracy. There has also been a grotesque rise in economic inequality in most of the world in this period; even in countries (like some in Latin America) where inequality has not sharply increased, its level often remains very high. The *World Inequality Report* data have shown that between 1980 and 2018 the share of national income going to the richest 1 percent has increased rapidly in China, India, the countries of North America, and Russia and more moderately in Europe. The International Monetary Fund's *World Economic Outlook Report* for April 2017 shows that labor share in national income has been by and large declining since at least the early 1990s in both advanced and developing economies. Such inequality is harmful to democracy, as it weakens the voice of the majority of workers and allows the elite to rig the democratic process (through various forms of influencing, media shaping, lobbying, and dominating campaign finance for business-friendly parties).

THE RISE OF POPULIST DEMAGOGUES

How do voters see these ongoing events? One of the most striking political phenomena in different parts of the world over the last decade or so has been the rise of so-called populism—in Brazil under Jair Bolsonaro, in Hungary under Viktor Orbán, in India under Narendra Modi, in the Philippines under Rodrigo Duterte, in Poland under the ruling Prawo i Sprawiedliwość (PiS) party, in Russia under Vladimir Putin, in Slovenia under Janez Janša, in Turkey under Recep Tayyip Erdoğan, in parts of the United Kingdom culminating in Brexit, in the United States under Donald Trump, and so on. There have also been strong populist opposition parties, as in France with Front National (now renamed Rassemblement National), in Italy with Lega Nord (and the Fratelli d'Italia), in Germany with Alternative für Deutschland (AfD),

in Spain with Vox, in Portugal with CHEGA and IL, and in Sweden
with Sverigedemokraterna. Most of these cases of populism come
mainly from the right. There have also been some cases of left-wing populism, particularly in Latin America (Argentina, Bolivia, Ecuador,
Mexico, Peru, and Venezuela), although—in reaction particularly to
what is called "the specter of Venezuela"—a hard right-wing movement
is also noticeable in parts of Latin America.

By *populism* different people, of course, mean different things. There
are differences in the use of the term *populism* even among academic
social scientists—between, say, economists and political scientists.
Economists associate it with short-termism, where long-term interests
of the economy are neglected often by policies of macroeconomic prof-
ligacy. But there is a distinct political science interpretation of populism, where a leader, supposed to embody the popular will, tramples
upon due process and the rules and institutions of representative
government. We are mainly concerned with the latter interpretation
here. This applies more directly in the cases of the right-wing populism mentioned above, though even in some left-wing cases there have
been violations of democratic procedures. (The Latin American left-
populist cases also provide some direct examples of the economists'
interpretation of populism.)

Populist upheavals have often upended or considerably weakened
the established centrist democratic parties. One frequently hears the
complaint that the latter have been insufficiently responsive to rising
inequality, with the rich getting richer, while the poor and the middle
classes have faced stagnation (or worse) in their incomes and standards
of living. In the general public discussion on populism it has been quite
common, both in media and in academia, to attribute its rise to the high
and increasing inequality. The widely noted 2011 protest movement
in New York, Occupy Wall Street (and similar Occupy movements
spawned by it elsewhere around that time), was directly a protest
against inequality and the top 1 percent in the income distribution,

though its organization style seems to have been inspired more by left-wing anarchism and sentiments for direct democracy than by right-wing populism. In Chile—off and on, several times over the last decade—protests have broken out against the stark inequalities and against the privatization of public services (protests on similar grounds also erupted in Colombia, Ecuador, and Peru in recent years). Though the Occupy movement soon fizzled out, the Chilean protest movement was protracted and resulted in a successful constitutional referendum, partly because the inequality protests were combined with widely perceived grievances about injustices flowing from privatized education and pension system. Recently a young left-wing leader who came to prominence during those protests won the presidential election.

Inequality does not seem to be the real substantive issue in many other populist agitations around the world. More often than not, when the demagogues tell the workers about the callousness of the political establishment to their economic plight, they enthusiastically rally to their banner and do not care that these leaders themselves often belong to the top 1 percent—as in the case of multimillionaires like Babiš, Erdoğan, Nigel Farage, Orbán, Putin, or Trump. In the United States prior to the rise of Trump there was the large antitaxation and anti-liberal-elite Tea Party movement stoked by an organization that was bankrolled by the billionaires Charles and David Koch. Sociologist Arlie Hochschild in her 2016 book *Strangers in Their Own Land* reports from her field survey of that movement in Louisiana that the poor white workers there are more resentful of minorities and immigrants than of the large petrochemical companies that have poisoned their land for decades. In India, Modi's Hindu fanatic supporters are more resentful of the usually much poorer Muslims than the crony capitalists that Modi seems cozy with. In general, the discontent that inequality may generate can be quite opaque and not always directed at the very rich, except rhetorically. Sociologists have often pointed out that the part of inequality that is salient to us is the contrast between our own lifestyle—and housing and school choices—and that of those who may be just above us. The inequality with the billionaires or the top 1 percent is too distant.

INSECURITY, MORE THAN INEQUALITY, AGITATES PEOPLE

It is arguable that, more than inequality, it is the rising insecurity that common people have faced over the last few decades that has fueled much of their dissatisfaction with established political parties and with the traditional rules and processes of representative democracy. Let me elaborate on this argument.

The insecurity I have in mind is of different kinds—much of it economic, but some of it also cultural, and even ecological and physical or existential insecurity in many contexts. The economic insecurity mainly refers to income and job insecurity. With increasing global integration, and particularly the rise of China, manufacturing jobs in advanced and also in some developing countries have been outsourced, and this has led to a sharp decline in many regional industries and economies. Whole areas have been blighted, and the local workers have found it difficult to change jobs or residence or adjust in other ways. There is widespread anxiety and despair.

The impact of "China shock" has now been documented and quantified for the US economy and some European economies. In the United States, the most well-known work, by David Autor and colleagues (2020), shows that in areas subject to larger import penetration there has been long-lasting decline in manufacturing employment and in relative earnings of low wage workers; and in the harder-hit areas there have been stronger political shifts in a right-wing direction (particularly if the areas have a sizable non-Hispanic white population). Also, in the

United States, the fabled land of high mobility of people, the actual extent of immobility has astonished many researchers, and geographic or place-based inequality turns out to be very high. Intergenerational mobility has also declined. It has been estimated by Raj Chetty and colleagues (2017) that for children born in 1940, there was a 90 percent chance that in their midthirties they'd earn an inflation-adjusted income higher than that of their parents; for the cohort born in 1980 that chance has declined substantially, thus darkening the aspirational horizon of a lot of middle-class families.

For Europe it is well known that support for Brexit has been particularly strong in the Midlands and Northern England, for Front National in deindustrializing areas of France, and for AfD in eastern Germany. In Europe, support for the European Union (EU) is often identified with support for economic integration and generally liberal policies. Using data from 63,417 electoral districts across all EU countries in the elections for the European Parliament, Lewis Dijkstra, Hugo Poelman, and Andrés Rodríguez-Pose (2020) show that voting for anti-EU parties is considerably higher in areas of industrial decline. Using European Social Survey data, Italo Colantone and Piero Stanig (2018) find that regions adversely affected by Chinese imports are less supportive of democratic institutions and less likely to hold liberal values.

There are no such detailed quantitative studies for India, but even there, it is easy to see that markets have been flooded by cheaper Chinese goods. This is not just in consumer electronics like cell phones and laptops; it has been widely noted that in religious festivals even idols of Indian gods and goddesses and the festive lights to illuminate them are made in China. China's larger scale of production—apart from subsidies and favored allocation of land and capital, in some cases—and India's worse infrastructure and worker skill levels make Indian domestic products often uncompetitive. Concomitantly, support for some protectionism and right-wing politics has increased in the last decade.

GLOBAL INTEGRATION INTERACTING
WITH AUTOMATION

At the same time, on a more general level it would be a mistake to look for a widespread backlash against globalization. There has recently been some decline in international trade largely due to supply chain disruption during the 2020 pandemic and the brewing geopolitical tension between China, Russia, and the United States, but as a fuel for the rise of populism one should not exaggerate its importance for a whole range of countries. Even at the height of populist upheavals, a survey of eighteen countries ("What the World Thinks About Globalization" 2016) reported in *The Economist* magazine suggested that the majority of respondents were quite positive on globalization in Denmark, Hong Kong, India, Malaysia, the Philippines, Thailand, Vietnam, among other places (if China had been included in the survey, it probably would have been on the same list). Support for globalization was low in Australia, France, the United Kingdom, and the United States. In the longer perspective, what we have seen is the expected fallout in rich countries from the decline in their domination for more than a century in international trade and investment and the growing assertiveness and weight of developing countries (particularly in Asia). An early 2020 survey carried out by YouGov Deutschland, as reported in Coka and Rausch (2020), just before the COVID-19 pandemic on attitudes toward globalization, in fifteen countries (some developed and some developing, including China), roughly confirms the 2016 findings. Support for globalization is stronger in developing than developed countries—strongest in the poorest country in the sample, Nigeria, and the weakest in France.

It is interesting to note that while people in rich countries are getting pessimistic about future generations being better off than the current generation, this is not the case in some of the low- or middle-income countries participating in the global integration process. For example, according to the Global Attitudes Survey of 2017 by the Pew Research

Center, as reported in Stokes (2017), in Europe and North America a median 60 percent of respondents (it is as high as 71 percent in France) believe that when children grow up they will be financially worse off than their parents; the corresponding numbers in India, Nigeria, the Philippines, and Indonesia are 12, 23, 24 and 26 percent, respectively.

In rich countries, in particular, what has interacted with the effect of global integration is the labor displacement effect of automation, digitization of tasks, robotization, and artificial intelligence. According to the Organisation for Economic Co-operation and Development (OECD 2020), about 46 percent of jobs in rich countries are either totally or partially (in terms of some tasks) likely to be subject to automation. Even in jobs where humans work with robots, many of the tasks are now increasingly performed at an intolerably accelerated, dehumanizing pace. Globalization and import penetration attract more public attention, as one can fix the blame on foreign companies and foreign government policies (and even though in most medium to large economies "nontradeables," like various services, form a big fraction of total output). But in many cases automation may have destroyed just as many jobs; this is particularly evident in the data where total value added increases even as employment falls.

This has political effects. Across eleven countries, using European Social Survey data, Zhen Jie Im and colleagues (2019) find that the likelihood of voting for radical Right parties is considerably higher for occupations affected by automation, and this effect is more pronounced for individuals reporting (very) low income security.

WHY A MOVE TO THE RIGHT, NOT THE LEFT?

A question that is pertinent here is why the recent job and income insecurity has been associated almost invariably with the rise of radical right-wing, but not left-wing, politics—except in some countries, like

Portugal, Spain, the Wallonia region of Belgium, and Mexico, where the Left has done better than the Right in reaction to the pressure for austerity policies to cope with the crisis. In Brazil and India the economic downturn after the financial crisis of 2007–2009 made the incumbent social democratic parties—the Partido dos Trabalhadores (PT) and the Congress Party, respectively—unpopular, along with charges of rampant corruption against them, and the anti-incumbent turn to the right-wing party is understandable. But in Hungary, the Netherlands, Poland, Sweden, and elsewhere the crisis (particularly in jobs and household debt) and the attendant austerity policies pushed voters mainly to the right rather than toward leftist parties advocating more redistribution.

One possible reason may be that, outside the United States, most right-wing parties (e.g., in France, Germany, India, or Poland) were not in favor of seriously weakening the preexisting worker welfare policies, which partly neutralized the attraction of leftist parties. In Poland the populist party PiS has been quite active in child assistance policies. In Turkey one signature policy of Erdoğan was to expand universal health care policy. Even on an explicitly redistributive issue, Thomas Piketty, in his book *Capital and Ideology*, reports the data from a survey of voters in the first round of 2017 presidential elections in France, that in response to a question about "taking from the rich and giving to the poor in order to achieve social justice," 46 percent of voters for Emmanuel Macron agreed that it was a good idea, but the percentage is significantly higher not just for the far-left voters for Jean-Luc Mélenchon (67 percent) but also for the right-wing voters for Marine Le Pen (61 percent). But the more important Left versus Right distinction in opinions may have to do with the fact that economic insecurity was often intertwined with cultural insecurity, which the Right was in a better position to exploit. Let us now examine this more closely.

CULTURAL INSECURITY

Cultural issues are, of course, different between rich and poor countries. There are more empirical studies available in Europe and the United States in recent years on how economic insecurity may have triggered cultural insecurity among certain sections of the population. In many places, particularly small towns and rural areas, there is evidence of the rise of cultural intolerance and majoritarian high-handedness, even violence, toward ethnic minorities and other nonstandard identity groups. With economic decline and depopulation in some areas, the local residents are anxious about preserving the identity of their traditional community (including its traditional status hierarchies). Psychologists point out that a sense of status insecurity and anxiety about one's diminished personal standing sometimes get expressed in aggression toward and intimidation of outside groups.

Related is the spreading anxiety about losing social / cultural status among the (lower) middle classes in many countries. Barbara Ehrenreich has vividly captured this for the United States in a book titled *Fear of Falling* (1989). This kind of social vertigo in an increasingly competitive world has alienated many from the mainstream political system. In India, with the widening of democracy in the last decades of the last century, the rise of the lower castes in the political hierarchy roused similar status anxiety in the middle classes. In Brazil similar effects were produced by the vigorous affirmative action programs pursued by the PT regime.

There is an interesting contrast in the dissatisfaction between right-wing and left-wing voters. Yann Algan and colleagues (2017) find that in the 2017 French presidential election, voters with low interpersonal trust were likely to vote for Le Pen. Even though left-wing voters for Mélenchon had similar low incomes and a sense of misery as the Le Pen voters, the former had more trust and wanted the government to address injustice. In the United States, Rafael Di Tella, Juan Dubra, and Alejandro Lagomarsino (2019) find that distrust in the government leads to skepticism about redistributive policies that the Left may advocate. Long-run data from the General Social Survey and the Pew Research Center suggest that interpersonal trust and trust in government have been at historically low levels in the United States in recent times. World Values Survey data, as reported in Ortiz-Ospina and Roser (2016), suggest that, in general, trust in government has been going down in OECD countries in recent years. Elsewhere, interpersonal trust is very low in highly unequal countries like Brazil, Chile, Colombia, Peru, and South Africa.

A part of the distrust of government is reflected in the hostility and suspicion against bureaucrats and politicians, and the "experts" and technocrats, in distant Brussels or Washington, DC, where the "deep state" has its supposed tentacles. "Take back control" is a popular slogan. In developing countries, officials and politicians are widely perceived to be corrupt—for example, a Pew Research Center survey in India in 2018, as reported in Devlin and Johson (2018), shows that two-thirds of respondents see politicians as corrupt—so skepticism about redistributive programs is not uncommon. In contrast, many religious charitable organizations are perceived as doing a good job in providing basic social services to the poor. In many cases these organizations are affiliates of populist right-wing parties (for detailed fieldwork evidence on the work of such grassroots affiliates in India, see Thachil [2014]). The contrast with frequently callous and corrupt government officials is clear, and poor voters may feel more attached to such populist religious parties on this ground than to left-wing parties promising redistributive social services through the usual bureaucratic channels.

The politically sensitive cultural issue that often divides the Right and Left is, of course, that of immigration. The early 2020 survey carried out by YouGov Deutschland, as reported in Halpin (2021), shows that in France, Germany, Mexico, and Russia a majority of respondents consider immigration to be a negative force. Support for anti-immigration parties in France and Italy are now quite high in opinion polls. (Even social democratic parties in Scandinavia have been compelled to adjust their policy toward immigration.) Immigration is, of course, both an economic and cultural issue, and its intensity varies with the immigrants' skill levels in labor market competition with native workers and their cultural distance from the local population.

But that it is primarily a cultural issue becomes apparent when one sees that the tension about immigrants remains even when people can be convinced that their net effect on the economy is often positive and that they are not a drain on the welfare budget. Of course, such convincing is itself a difficult task, as there is a wide gulf between popular perception and reality on the numbers involved: Albert Alesina, Armando Miano, and Stefanie Stantcheva (2019) show from survey data that the proportion of migrants in the population is perceived to be two to three times as large as the actual levels in the United States and western Europe. The false stereotypes and generally adverse perception is higher in areas where immigrants are fewer than in big cities and urban hubs, where immigrants mostly are, and populist politicians usually get more support in the former areas. In Germany, for example, the anti-immigrant extreme right-wing AfD gets more support in the eastern part of the country, where there are very few immigrants. Yotam Margalit (2019) shows, from a number of studies, that there is negative attitude to immigrants even among workers whose jobs are not directly affected. It is possible that the anxiety arising even from nonlocal stories of economic insecurity and job churning on TV and social media heightens the general sense of insecurity.

In addition, there is special aversion to Muslim immigrants, particularly in Europe—Muslim masons face more hate and discrimination than do Polish plumbers. This is partly because of the large cultural gulf in social norms with the natives, partly the stereotypical Islamophobic association of all Muslims with international terrorism, and partly because of an exaggerated looming sense of massive numbers of Muslim immigrants in Europe from nearby countries taking over—which is, for example, captured in the novel *Submission* by the French writer Michel Houellebecq on a dystopian speculation about a time when France has become an Islamic state. There are accounts by right-wing intellectuals of what is called the Great Replacement (of the indigenous by immigrants). In French politics, even Macron and his ministers are fuming against "Islamo-leftism" (a term for liberal appeasement of Muslims, and also a familiar trope for supporters of Modi or Trump), and Le Pen has softened her party's economic policies (now not so much against the euro, and even calling for "green reindustrialization") while hardening its stance on Islam and immigration.

In southeastern Europe the populists sometimes invoke selective historical memory. Christian Ochsner and Felix Rosel (2019) point out how in recent elections the right-wing parties in Austria stoked the memory of Ottoman pillaging around Vienna in 1529 and 1683 and harvested votes more in the previously pillaged than nonpillaged municipalities, in an area where there was no difference in anti-Muslim sentiment between the two kinds of municipalities before. (During the Bosnian War, such stoking by ethnic group leaders of long-dormant hostilities between Serbs and Muslims was quite common.)

Such anti-Muslim sentiment and the practice of stoking historical resentment among Hindu nationalists has become quite rampant in India. The nationalists have also created a false sense that Hindus are soon to be outnumbered by the Muslims due to the latter's higher fertility rates, even though Hindus constitute about 80 percent of the population and the fertility rates of Muslims in areas of higher levels of mass education (e.g., Kerala) are significantly lower than those of Hindus in less educated areas (e.g., Uttar Pradesh). What is overlooked is that, more than religious affiliation, a major determinant of fertility rates is the level of a mother's education, and that the latter often depends on vigorous public education policies of the local government (as in Kerala). In general there is a manufactured sense of Hindu victimhood, running on the same lines as ideas about white victimhood and a loss of entitlement that white supremacists in Europe or the United States have created. The Hindu militant cultural organization Rashtriya Swayamsevak Sangh not only provides the main political leadership in the ruling party but is also reported to have infiltrated some sections of the military and the police.

Religious / cultural majoritarianism is also the main fuel for rightwing populist parties in other developing countries like Brazil and Turkey. In Turkey the secular-religious divide has polarized people for many decades, and the association of the secular with the military, which often brutally persecuted religious people, as well as the Left, made some prodemocratic forces initially side with the Justice and Development Party (Adalet ve Kalkınma Partisi; AKP) led by Erdoğan, which rallied many of the poor and moderately religious people. But over time the party became more Islamist and hostile to non-Muslims, Kurds, and atheists and gave up on democratic pretensions. Its organizations and networks, however, were widespread, including the membership of Islamic trade unions, and its large housing and other construction projects and health policy had popular support. (Very recently, Erdoğan's mismanagement of the economy has caused some disaffection among the poor).

In Brazil, evangelists, particularly from Pentecostal churches, succeeded in mobilizing support for the populist leader, Bolsonaro, among many poor people. Some military groups offer powerful backing, too, as Bolsonaro is one of their own. The police have also been largely militarized. In the virulent culture wars raged by these Bolsonaro supporters much of the fomenting of hate and associated hate crimes are directed against cultural minorities—black people, women, followers of African religions, and LGBTQ people. (Of late, Bolsonaro's gross mismanagement of the pandemic has led to a slump in his popularity.)

RESENTMENT OF THE ELITE

Those who consider inequality the source of populism point out that the populists are anti-elite. But the right-wing populists' target is often not the financial elite but the cultural elite. In Europe, India, Turkey, the United States, and elsewhere, the perceived appeasement of minorities—assumed to be implicit in the liberal support for minority rights—fosters resentment among the majority, which finds the liberal rhetoric of diversity and political correctness condescending if not outright threatening. Conversely, a Modi or a Trump's thinly veiled rantings or spewing of venom, taken as raw antiestablishment spontaneity ("He tells it like it is"), energize this base. In Hochschild's book (2016), her white working-class respondents in Louisiana sense that all demographic groups other than theirs receive sympathy from liberals. Hochschild quotes a gospel singer, an avid Rush Limbaugh fan, saying, "Oh, liberals think that Bible-believing Southerners are ignorant, backward, rednecks, losers. They think we're racist, sexist, homophobic, and maybe fat." A Tea Party enthusiast claims, "People think we're not good people if we don't feel sorry for blacks and immigrants and Syrian refugees. . . . But I am a good person and I don't feel sorry for them."

In different parts of the world, ethnic and cultural minorities are often oppressed and pushed to the wall by the leaders of majoritarian parties who, as I have noted, succeed in stoking in the majority communities feelings of victimhood and being under siege. In India (or Turkey) one will hear Hindu (or Muslim) fanatics ranting about the danger they face from terrorist Muslims (or Kurds); in Hungary one will hear about being deluged by (largely nonexistent) immigrants. As a result, there is now considerable tension between the politics of electoral mobilization and the procedural aspects of democracy. Mobilized followers do not care much about the procedural niceties of a liberal order. They often show impatience with the encumbrances of due process and affirmative action. They hanker for strong leaders who can embody the will of the people, surpass those encumbrances, and provide seductively simple solutions to problems. The organizational norms of traditional political parties that once disciplined mass fanaticism are being cast aside; voters are choosing political outsiders, or, within established political parties, leaders who defy traditionalists (like the bullying shambolic showman Boris Johnson in the British Tory Party), or (as in the US primaries) the more radical sections of the party get more voice. In some populist leaders brazenness, incivility, and in-your-face aggressiveness activate cultural tribalism and are taken as a sign of "authenticity," in contrast with the duplicitous, wily, and politically correct style of established leaders. Even when a centrist leader like Emmanuel Macron wins, as in the April 2022 election, large numbers consider him aloof, as reflected in the substantial vote share for Le Pen and the low voter turnout.

Among some recent writers there is a general critique of liberal modernity, popular with postmodernists and cultural theorists, that resonates ideologically with the turn toward populism. This critique usually associates modernity with cutthroat capitalism, and the ravages of imperialism with a presiding technocratic nation-state. It traces the poison all the way back to the Enlightenment, even though it should be pointed out that Karl Marx and Mao Zedong are as much the children of this modernity as are Adam Smith and Milton Friedman. This critique of modernity is now quite familiar from the reading lists of any self-respecting cultural studies department. Here I shall confine myself to its exposition in Pankaj Mishra's *Age of Anger* (2017), in which the critique is directly related to the populist anger that concerns us here.

Going back to the eighteenth century, Mishra recalls Jean-Jacques Rousseau's romanticist reaction to the Enlightenment's rationalist narrative of unyielding progress, finding a reflection of that reaction in today's illiberal challenge, from the angry worker in the US Rust Belt all the way to the Islamist suicide bomber. *Ressentiment,* born out of "an intense mix of envy and sense of humiliation and powerlessness," is undermining civic society. We are made to believe that *Homo economicus,* in its hyperrational pursuit of greed and self-interest, is the culprit.

For all of the faults of capitalism (and economics, for that matter), I think this is too sweeping a judgment. In trying to explain too much, it actually explains very little. Contrary to Mishra's image of an angry East reacting to the destabilizing effects of Western capitalism, this rage appears to be less intense in those parts of the East (including East, South, and Southeast Asia) where capitalist growth has been relatively successful, than in North Africa and West Asia, where capitalist growth has been stunted and economic misery has been accentuated by corrupt political tyranny. The highly popular Arab Spring, soon snuffed out, was a rebellion not against Western liberalism but against domestic tyranny and youth unemployment. The traditional Islamists seem disturbed less by the rational pursuit of money (Islam has nothing against profit seeking) than by the collusion between domestic and foreign oligarchies. In fighting the "crusaders," the Islamists try to build an apparatus with all its modernist technomilitary paraphernalia.

Contrary to Mishra's view, there is an intellectual tradition that suggests that economic interests can in fact tame human passions. In *The General Theory of Employment, Interest and Money* (1936), John Maynard Keynes writes, "Dangerous human proclivities can be canalized into comparatively harmless channels by the existence of opportunity for money-making and private wealth, which, if they cannot be satisfied in this way, may find their outlet in cruelty, the reckless pursuit of personal power and authority, and other forms of self-aggrandizement." Albert O. Hirschman's *The Passions and the Interests* (1977) has a more nuanced discussion of the relationship between interests and passions. Yet both Keynes and Hirschman were talking about earlier times in Europe. Today, when the opportunities for moneymaking have opened up in countries such as China and India, passions are channeled by the ruling party into the service of a national aggrandizement that capitalist growth has at last made possible.

Of course, in recent years the gulf between the working class and the liberal elite has widened. The blue-collar working-class supporters of populist demagogues are often older, less educated, and residents of small towns and rural areas. They are socially more conservative and their life is centered around often decaying local communities. The elites, meanwhile, have become isolated by effectively segregating themselves in large gentrified cities, marrying within their class, and adopting mostly professional occupations and lifestyles. This liberal professional elite is more cosmopolitan in outlook; they are "globalists" in Trump's pejorative term, or "citizens of nowhere," as described by Theresa May, the former UK conservative prime minister. In Western countries this liberal elite has provided much of the support base for the type of politics practiced by Tony Blair, the Clintons, Emmanuel Macron, or Barack Obama, which has driven away significant numbers of the white working class disillusioned about social democratic parties (we'll come back to this in chapter 6). The elite politics have often connived at some pruning of the welfare state and public services, macroeconomic austerity policies, trade and financial liberalization, and openness to immigration and to the increasing diversity of identity groups (based on race, gender, or sexual orientation)—all of which have in one way or another alienated many among workers.

As I have mentioned, anti-elitist populist wrath in developing countries is similarly not against the financial elite. In India, for example, Modi, the leader of the Bharatiya Janata Party (BJP) is, as I have noted, quite cozy with billionaire businessmen, some of whom get special state favors for their companies—in particular in the terms for loans from public banks, relaxed terms for default on such loans, tax concessions, and waivers from or the dilution of regulations, including those for protecting the environment and forest people. In return the BJP gets corporate donations, many times larger than all the other political parties combined, through a process that was always murky but has recently been made murkier by a system of electoral bonds on which there is hardly any requirement for disclosure. Crony oligarchy is the prevalent mode in the economic sphere. Meanwhile the Gini index of wealth inequality in India (measured from household survey data that usually understate such inequality) has almost reached the same range as in Latin America, which alongside West Asia is usually considered to be the most unequal region in the world. The top 1 percent in India holds nearly one-third of all wealth. Politically, as Gilles Verniers and Christophe Jaffrelot (2020) show, the BJP, in spite of its rhetoric of inclusion, primarily recruits its parliamentary candidates from the traditional elite (its upper-caste representation is substantially more than that of other parties) and from strong local and regional business networks.

Populist wrath is instead focused against the liberal cultural elite, which is supposed to be "soft" on minorities, and particularly Muslims. Muslims are among the poorest groups in India, often discriminated against by the majority Hindu population in jobs, housing, and social interaction; they are victims of hate crimes and violence perpetrated by vigilante mobs, highly underrepresented in politics (while they are 14 percent of the population, they hold only about 4 percent of seats in the Indian Parliament). Yet the BJP has succeeded in creating a false narrative of Muslim perfidy (with Muslim-majority Pakistan next door as the perpetual bogeyman), citing the history of Muslim conquest many centuries back and recent cases of international terrorism and illegal immigration. In his campaigns Modi has invoked what he calls Hindu anger. As we have seen, this trope of false victimhood, manufactured resentment, and the imaginary danger of being outnumbered often works. The BJP has figured out that stoking intercommunity tension helps the party mobilize majoritarian impulses and consolidate large numbers of low-caste Hindu votes for a party of mainly the socioeconomic elite, somewhat like the Republican Party in the United States serving the interests of the business elite, while stoking culture wars to consolidate party votes among the socially conservative lower classes.

Even though the right-wing populist parties in both India and Turkey draw upon religious majoritarianism, there is an important difference in the development of the party support base in the two countries. In Turkey the poor, the less educated, and the rural middle classes were always major supporters of the AKP, and over time the party succeeded in mobilizing a more cross-class coalition. In India the BJP was initially mainly a party of Hindu upper castes, traders, and urban middle classes; only in recent years has it succeeded in making alliances with some middle and lower castes and appealed to some poor people through its Hindu nationalist slogans, national security alarms, and, in particular, Modi's personal oratorical discourse of affinity with the aspiring groups coming up from below, resentful of the Westernized liberal elite. Demonizing Muslims as potential traitors and terrorists served the BJP's cause. Similarly, in Brazil, Bolsonaro's main support base was the urban elite and middle classes, alienated by the pro-poor welfare and affirmative action programs of the earlier PT government, but it succeeded in mobilizing the poor through campaigns against crime in the favelas (against so-called bandidos) and through evangelical appeals. In India and Brazil most major metropolitan cities have mainly supported the right-wing populist parties, whereas in Turkey, as in the United States, the major metropolitan cities largely voted against them. One difference between Brazil and India, however, is that the religious and cultural majoritarianism of the BJP in India is more organized and disciplined than in the case of Bolsonaro's party. The media, judiciary, and civil society organizations have also been much more resistant in Brazil than in India. This may be one of the reasons the move to the right is likely to be more durable in India.

THE TOXIC ROLE OF SOCIAL MEDIA

It is now well known that in propagating false narratives, spewing ethnic vitriol, sharpening polarization, and spreading conspiracy theories the internet and social media have played a crucial role. All over the world the right-wing troll armies have been much more effective in spreading their message than the Left has been in countering the damage and spreading its own message. Regulated more lightly than traditional media, capable of reaching people more directly, and with algorithms that reproduce narratives and send them to like-minded people, the social media have been instrumental in creating vast echo chambers of falsehoods and stereotypes, insulated from checks and balances or correcting narratives. The platforms have also provided a new and easy way for extremists to recruit and crowdsource funds. Populist governments, recognizing all of this, sometimes even hire private firms that specialize in spreading disinformation and discrediting their opponents.

In a gathering of the party's social media volunteers in 2018, Amit Shah—the then-party chief of the BJP, currently the home minister of India—boasted (as quoted in the *Wire,* September 26, 2018), "We are capable of delivering any message we want to the public, whether sweet or sour, true or fake. We can do this work only because . . . of our WhatsApp groups. That is how we (a)re able to make this viral." In an op-ed in the *New York Times,* Shoshana Zuboff (2020) described the social media platforms as "hyper-velocity global blood streams into which anyone may introduce a dangerous virus without a vaccine." There is also a lot of evidence now that false stories spread much faster than true ones, and to a much larger number of users—and the more outrageous tales spread even more rapidly (and the tech companies of social media have a vested interest in virality). Hunt Allcott and Matthew Gentzkow (2017) find in their data that in the three months before the 2016 presidential election in the United States, false stories on Facebook favoring Trump were shared about thirty million times, while false stories favoring Clinton were shared eight million times. As early as 1710, Jonathan Swift had said, "Falsehood flies, and truth comes limping after it."

Conspiracy theories create an atmosphere of suspicion about established institutions and of lurking danger, for which the populist leaders are self-acclaimed guarantors of protection. A 2019 survey by YouGov and the Cambridge Globalism Project of twenty-six thousand people in twenty-five countries asked respondents whether they believe there is "a single group of people who secretly control events and rule the world together." Thirty-seven percent in the United States replied that this is "definitely or probably true"; the numbers were 45 percent for Italy, 55 percent for Spain, and 78 percent for Nigeria. Trust in standard democratic procedures and institutions is bound to suffer in such circumstances. No wonder that a Pew Research Center survey of thirty-four countries in 2019 found that a median of 52 percent of respondents are dissatisfied with democracy in their country. A more recent study of 160 countries by Foa et al. (2020) for the Centre for the Future of Democracy at Cambridge University finds that, worldwide, an average of 58 percent of citizens are dissatisfied with democracy (it was 39 percent in 2005); this is particularly the case among the young.

In this chapter I have associated the rise of right-wing populism and the decline of faith in democratic institutions and practices in different parts of the world with the rise in economic and cultural insecurity. Let us note here that other kinds of insecurity in recent years may also be involved. In several ways, issues of even physical or sheer existential insecurity have been uppermost in many minds. These include a rise in terrorism (particularly since September 11, 2001); war and civil strife; ecological catastrophes arising from extreme climate events like hurricanes, forest fires, floods, and mudslides; and long-running problems like the rise in sea levels, overfishing, deforestation, soil erosion, and desertification. Such problems have displaced many livelihoods and led to mass migration—the World Bank has estimated that by midcentury about 143 million people in Latin America, South Asia, and sub-Saharan Africa will be climate change refugees. An increase in crimes (particularly against women, their numbers exceeding the simple increase in reporting) has further heightened anxiety. And all of this has been exacerbated by the COVID-19 pandemic, which upended life and livelihoods in 2020 and beyond for masses of people. The age of insecurity continues to cast its pall over society and polity all over the world.

2

Taking Back Control

BACK TO THE COMMUNITY?

As I mentioned in Chapter 1, one persistent call in recent populist or anti-liberal-establishment movements has been to take back control from distant politicians and officials, restoring autonomy and control to the community level. Critics also express disdain for the advisers to those officials, the experts and other professionals, who come across as privileged meritocrats and rootless cosmopolitans out of touch with local realities and sensibilities. At the emotional level there is, particularly prominent among those with a conservative bent, a yearning for community-embedded identity at a time of fast-paced and disorienting changes in technology and society.

The idea of going back to the community is part of an old debate in social and political movements. For example, in the middle decades of nineteenth-century Russia, the Narodniks and anarchists, with their ideas of going back to the peasant community as the prime repository of the Slavic soul and as the main seedbed of social change, contended with Russian liberals on the one hand and Marxists on the other. In India in the first half of the twentieth century, Mahatma Gandhi, an admirer of Leo Tolstoy who in his 1909 book *Hind Swaraj* had described himself as an "enlightened anarchist," harked back to the rural community as the central focus of social reorganization in the struggle for freedom. By contrast, Jawaharlal Nehru and what later came to be known as the Congress Socialist Party were advocating socialist industrialization, while pro-business groups mainly around the city of Bombay were advocating some form of market liberalism.

THE COMMUNITY IN RELATION TO
THE MARKET AND THE STATE

These contending ideological positions can be traced to the different weights one gives to the foundational values of liberty, equality, and fraternity enunciated even earlier, at the time of the French Revolution. They are evident too in the ideas that evolved somewhat later about the alternately conflicting and other times more complementary social coordination mechanisms of the state, the market, and the community in the striving for those foundational values. I shall discuss these issues further in Chapter 6, but let me note here some of the possible contradictions as well as complementarities among these values or mechanisms, particularly in the context of the community. How communities can get ravaged by the impact of (global) markets is widely acknowledged. Take, for example, Belgium's Jean-Pierre and Luc Dardenne's feature films on the lives of common working people in the deindustrialized parts of western Europe, or Michael Moore's films about those in the Rust Belt in the US Midwest. In India comparable struggles appear in various well-known books, like *The Unquiet Woods* by Ramachandra Guha (2000), that show how erstwhile community-held forests have been ravaged both by the state (colonial and postcolonial) and markets and how peasants have sought to resist.

On the other hand, there can be meaningful complementary relations between the community and the market or the state. Community organizations can productively use market processes, like the partnerships between businesses and nongovernmental organizations in Bangladesh that have improved access to telecommunications in rural areas; and, of course, many agricultural and dairy cooperatives in Denmark or India run by local communities have been major business successes. Similarly, there are impressive examples of community-state cooperation, as in many parent-teacher associations in US public schools or joint forest management between the Indian government's Forest Service and local communities. In this chapter we shall examine diverse analytical aspects of the role of communities, going beyond the simpler generalizations of community enthusiasts and skeptics.

Community complaints against the depredations of the market and the state have abounded in recent years. Global markets and the mobility of capital have required standardization and the harmonization of local rules and regulations, which some communities feel are ironing out their local distinctiveness and eroding personalized networks reliant on proximity. Large corporate firms at the same time have crowded out small businesses, captured state power in democracies through strong lobbies and copious election funding, and weakened labor organizations, thus depressing labor share in the economy, making many livelihoods precarious and many ordinary people suspicious of markets.

State-provided public services, which are supposed to relieve the harshness of the market, are everywhere riddled with bureaucratic indifference, malfeasance, and resistance to reform, while the rich are increasingly seceding from those public services, further eroding the services' support base. In developing countries, the public delivery of social services is often so dismal (thanks to inept, corrupt, or truant officials), and attempts at reform are so often resisted by vested interests (including public-sector unions), that, as I noted in Chapter 1, the image of voluntary community organizations (including charitable religious institutions, be they Christian, Hindu, or Muslim) doing small-scale work to try to fill in the gaps is often much better than that of the state.

Even when the state's delivery mechanisms work reasonably well, the projects often do not engage with the people but simply treat them as passive objects of the development process. In rich countries, communities have sometimes rejected negotiations conducted over their heads by corporate and city officials to help investment in the community— as in the case of the failed Amazon investment proposal for the borough of Queens in New York City in 2019.

THE COMMUNITY AS ANCHOR

Ideologically, conservatives drawing upon community traditions have tried to deflate the universalistic pretentions of liberalism. They say that, for many people, liberalism, in privileging individual autonomy and freedom, often leaves a social and emotional vacuum that conservatives are more adept at filling. There is something deeper involved here than the simple fact that many people feel more comfortable with the moral certitudes that conservatives usually offer in contrast to the prickly skepticism of the liberals. In his book *On Human Nature* (2017), the conservative philosopher Roger Scruton was on to something when he distinguished between the liberal individual, self-possessed in her autonomous decisions about consent, contract, and trade, and the conservative individual who endows her life with meaning mainly through embeddedness in a community with established traditions. Communitarian philosophers like Charles Taylor have criticized what they call the "atomism" of the libertarian concept of the self, and suggested that the moral commitments that define our identity and meaning may arise from the social world in which we are located. Gandhi, though he respected the liberal emphasis on autonomy and self-realization, sought to balance it with the communitarian emphasis on moral duty arising from membership in one's own community.

At the political level, and in the day-to-day democratic process, political parties that used to be viable mediators between the state and
society are now in some decay all over the world. The regular political-
organizational channels that articulate demand and help resolve conflicts are thus clogged. At the global level there is also a general feeling
that, in facing the environmental challenges, both the state and the
market have failed us. Even in the community management of local
environmental resources—in forestry, fishing, irrigation, and management of grazing lands—rampant encroachments by private business
and by overreaching and collusive state officials have played havoc in
many parts of the world. The result is widespread disillusionment with
both the market and the state. In such a situation some chastened liberals are turning to the local community to provide an anchor for
democratic institutions and solidarity.

Communitarians and sociologists have, of course, argued for this
over many decades, but economists have usually been skeptical,
emphasizing that community loyalties can be a drag on the efficient
allocation of resources and on the productivity that arises from mobile and footloose labor and capital. They put a greater emphasis on
anonymous competition than on social cooperation. The only recipient of the Nobel Prize in Economics who has extensively worked on
community-based institutions of cooperation, Elinor Ostrom, was a
political scientist, not an economist. When in the early 1990s I linked
up with her in connection with my work on community institutions
in the local commons of developing countries, she expressed bewil-
derment at why so few of my fellow economists were interested in
such issues.

This is changing now. More economists, persuaded by the ubiq-
uity of both market and state failures, are turning to the community
as the "third pillar" of society and economy—as a very sensible recent book by Raghuram Rajan (2019) has called it. Policy suggestions
involving devolution of power to local community associations, or to

village councils and municipal administrations, now abound in the economic governance literature for both rich and poor countries.

The main economic arguments in favor of such devolution include: (1) a better utilization of local information, ingenuity and initiative, particularly in the targeting and implementation of public projects, which distant technocrats cannot easily mobilize or sustain; (2) the procedures of trust, coordination, and social sanctions of defaulters that undergird local social contracts—all of which become weaker as the domain expands beyond small local communities so that exit becomes easier and social norms get diluted; and (3) a desire to keep under control the inequalities that large-scale agglomeration and network externalities inevitably generate (when talented and skilled people gravitate toward one another in a small area or entity, others elsewhere fall behind and suffer the consequences of the brain drain).

Examples are many, in rich and poor countries alike, of devolution leading to better decisions, from the point of view of efficiency, equity, and fitness to specific local conditions and challenges. Technological changes have now made it administratively somewhat easier for lower levels of government to handle certain tasks, just as after the pandemic more people now have the opportunity to work from remote areas and connect up with distant markets and offices. Local politics and governance also provide a good training ground for future democratic leaders at the national level. And in a world of rampant ethnic conflicts and separatist movements, devolution of power can diffuse social and political tensions and ensure local cultural and political autonomy.

THE COSTS OF LOCALISM

But liberals should also beware of communitarian romanticism. Compared to central entities, where many rival groups contend and are often forced to compromise, small local community institutions may be more susceptible to capture by local overlords, oligarchs, and majoritarian tyrants. Think of white supremacists in the localities of the US South, the tyranny of dominant castes in Indian villages, or the Mafia's capture of local institutions in Sicily. In all of these cases, outside intervention has been necessary to relieve institutionalized systems of local oppression. In India, during the struggle for freedom, important social thinkers like Mahatma Gandhi and Rabindranath Tagore emphasized the centrality of the village community, but B. R. Ambedkar, the leader of a marginalized and oppressed group (who as one of the founding fathers of the Constitution of India tried to do something about that oppression through liberal-constitutional means), described the Indian village community as "a sink of localism, a den of ignorance, narrow-mindedness and communalism" on November 4, 1948, during the Constituent Assembly Debates. When there is such a community failure for socially marginalized groups, the anonymity of the market or an intervention by the distant state, with its impersonal legal procedures, may be welcome.

Of course, communitarians point out that the state may try to use laws to relieve the oppression of one social group by another, but law is a blunt and sometimes ineffective instrument for social change. State laws against racial discrimination in the United States, or oppression of low-caste people (the Burakumin in Japan or the Dalits in India) have been at best very slow in removing those social ills. Social movements and community reforms may work better than passing state laws that remain little more than an aspiration. Yet while this means the state may not be sufficient for reform, it may still be necessary to initiate or catalyze changes of oppressive practices within the community.

At a somewhat less oppressive level of associational life, all of us are familiar with the problems that arise from insiders having too much control in local bodies for zonal restrictions or professional licensing. We are familiar with "not in my backyard" resistance to new projects that, for example, would have built denser but more vibrant cities with fewer scattered suburbs in the United States. (Even liberal but expensive cities like San Francisco are divided on the issue of public housing projects.) And it's well known that school financing based on local property taxes can work against the interests of the poor and disadvantaged. Decentralization can thus exacerbate intercommunity inequality. When power is devolved, communities with initial advantages build on them and advance faster. Richer areas may also have more clout or lobbying power with higher authorities who allocate relevant resources. In a study of the distributional effects of decentralization across municipalities on educational quality in Argentine secondary schools, Sebastian Galiani, Paul Gertler, and Ernesto Schargrodsky (2008) find that schools in poorer municipalities fell further behind, while those in better-off areas improved.

Then there are related issues like externalities and spillovers, where local control mechanisms are inadequate, as in the case of upstream deforestation causing flooding and soil erosion in downstream communities. Intracommunity economic inequality can also have an adverse impact on trust and cooperation. For instance, in my empirical work on south Indian (irrigation) water communities, I have found statistical evidence that—across villages, when land is more unequally distributed—farmers' cooperation on the resolution of water conflicts breaks down more easily.

The small scale of communities can also be a disadvantage when they face what are called covariate risks (for example, when natural disasters or local market mishaps affect most members of a local community simultaneously). Risk pooling to keep insurance costs under control in such cases requires supralocal involvement and work at a larger scale. Small scale is also a disadvantage when infrastructure investments require raising large amounts of external finance. Investment from outside in active collaboration with local community authorities to make communities attractive for new business opportunities and to rebuild their often decrepit local infrastructure may be imperative.

TRADE-OFFS BETWEEN INSURANCE AND FREEDOM

Liberal democrats also face a dilemma when considering social insurance against risks and financial hardship provided at the community level. On the one hand, kinship groups in traditional communities often provide their members with consumption credit that is otherwise difficult to procure, as well as emotional support, at times of emergency need. They may also offer small loans for regular business needs or job referrals for migrating members and may insure against idiosyncratic risks. These useful functions and reciprocal obligations make such group ties quite resilient (and help some ethnic business groups to succeed where entrepreneurial opportunities and capital are scarce).

Such group obligations can actually serve even better than market or government contracts, since the latter ultimately depend for contract enforcement on costly third-party (legal-juridical) verification and arbitration. In the case of face-to-face communities, breaches of agreements are more easily observable and negotiable, while social sanctions act as a powerful deterrent to breaking them in the first place. There are many stories of how Chinese lineage-based business families negotiate billions of dollars' worth of real estate deals in Hong Kong without any formal contracts for raising money from inside those groups and police any potential breaches mainly internally. Caste-based Gujarati migrant families have captured the motel business in large parts of the United States in similar fashion.

Of course, as the scale of economic activity expands and the need for external finance and professional management talent become imperative, family businesses face increasing constraints. John Shuhe Li (2003) has expressed the dilemma in terms of economic costs: "relation-based" systems of business governance may have low fixed costs (given the social community relationships among parties and the avoidance of elaborate legal-juridical and verification costs of more "rule-based" systems), but they may have high and rising marginal costs (particularly of monitoring and finance raising) as business expansion involves successively weaker relational links.

On the social side of the ledger, the benefits of community bonds come with a palpable cost for individuals. The price of social help and insurance is the group's authority over members' freedoms. Traditional extended families or kinship groups can be quite authoritarian in their treatment—particularly of younger and female members. The latter, for example, have to accept many restrictions on their choice of work associates and marriage partners, sanctions on departures from due deference to the aged leaders, and injunctions on sharing the benefits from individual efforts and innovations.

Let us examine the case of old-age support. In traditional communities, children have the social obligation to look after their parents in their old age. The community keeps a watchful eye so that as the children grow up they do not stray too far away from community controls. A liberal may actually prefer the state and market alternatives (social security plus financial market products like annuities) to the community-provided support system obligating children. More generally, in such societies (even when they are democratic), group rights often take precedence over individual rights: a person's freedom of expression can be restricted if some group claims it takes offense at her expression or speech. The individual rights that liberalism emphasizes may sometimes lead to violation of community norms; in this sense, liberty and fraternity may be in serious conflict. One can see this conflict in complex thinkers like Gandhi, who as an ardent champion of the local community was less warm to liberalism (particularly if it came without serious limits on competition and on the individual's autonomy of desire and needs) and egalitarianism.

In his book *Two Cheers for Anarchism,* the political scientist James C. Scott endorses many of the thoughtful ideas of great anarchist thinkers of the past (like Mikhail Bakunin or Pierre-Joseph Proudhon) on the independent self-organizing power of individuals and small communities for informal coordination without hierarchy, but he recognizes that the state is not always the enemy of freedom and that the relative equality that is necessary for small-group coordination and mutuality can often only be guaranteed through the state.

DEMOCRATIC PROCESS VERSUS COMMUNITY PARTICIPATION

Another conflict arises in the context of two other aspects of liberal democracy—the procedural and the participatory. The former concerns due process and respect for minority rights, which majoritarian communities often tend to ride roughshod over. These communities, in their impatience with institutional rules and procedures, are often complicit in their leaders' illiberal undermining of the institutional insulation or independence of the judiciary, police, and civil service, particularly in developing countries where these institutions are already weak. They emphasize instead winning elections through majoritarian mobilization. I will discuss this further in Chapter 5.

Of course, enthusiasts for participatory politics often complain about the failures of representative democracy, as the representatives tend to come to them only at election time and meanwhile delegate vital issues to unelected elite experts or an insulated technocracy. If both the procedural and participatory aspects of liberal democracy are to be given their due weight, one clearly has to strike a balance between the need for evidence- and knowledge-based governance, which is indispensable in many complex situations (as became evident in the differential attitude of people to warnings by doctors and epidemiologists during the pandemic), and the need for frequent and meaningful checks ensuring that decision-makers are accountable to the people. In poor countries, even when there are vigorous local governments, a serious financial problem for local accountability is that many local areas are too poor to have elastic sources of revenue. So, even if they have some political power, it is limited by their dependence on money coming from above. Accountability is thus separated from financial responsibility. In such a context the standard presumption of the economic literature on fiscal federalism—that people can vote with their feet in the face of different bundles of tax and public expenditure in different areas—does not quite apply. Residents of rural communities in poor countries live face-to-face, and social norms sharply distinguish "outsiders" from "insiders," especially with respect to entitlement to community services.

Recent experience with programs intended to enhance community participation in developing countries has shown only limited gains in many areas, and particularly in those with entrenched inequality. Lending institutions like the World Bank have long emphasized participatory programs like community-driven development in public goods projects. While several such programs have delivered moderately successfully to the poor, it is not always clear that the local institutional setups, deficient in empowerment of the poor, have measurably or durably changed. Yet there is now scattered evidence of local deliberative democracy sprouting up in different parts of the world and showing results—if not always in policy outcome at least in the process of claims to dignity and discursive demands for accountability. The evidence is not just from the town halls of rich countries or citizens' assemblies in France and Ireland deliberating on important issues of the day, or participatory budgeting in progressive Brazilian cities, but even from high-inequality, low-literacy villages in India—as Paromita Sanyal and Vijayendra Rao's book *Oral Democracy* (2018) shows for a fairly large sample of village assemblies in South India.

On the issue of expertise local or indigenous knowledge may be enough for the management of some problems, but certainly not for all. When someone in the village is seriously ill, the community leaders may send for the traditional healers in the neighborhood, but one may be safer in the hands of experts in the hospital in the nearby town (provided by the market or the state). On an administrative level, the municipal authority may be well placed to provide street cleaning or garbage collection, but for power generation and transmission, bulk supplies of clean water, public sanitation, or developing a school curriculum or digital connectivity it will often need outside help and expertise from the upper levels of the state and the market.

COMMUNITY NORMS AND EXCLUSIVITY

Beyond administrative accountability to the grass roots, the case for community ultimately depends on the salience of common cultural bonds and norms for a healthy liberal society. Here the cultural gulf between blue-collar workers and the liberal professional elite has become particularly wide in recent years, as was noted in Chapter 1. Labor organizations, instead of serving only as narrow wage-bargaining platforms or lobbies, can play a special role in bridging this gulf. They may take an active role in local cultural life, involving the neighborhood community and religious organizations, as they used to do in some European and Latin American countries, thus helping tame and transcend some nativist passions. (We will come back to this theme in Chapter 9.)

A return to community norms and cultural visions without encouraging exclusivity and barriers is, of course, an extremely delicate task. Success in this will vary from one area to another, often depending on organizations and leaders. It is often the case that dislocations due to market or technological disruptions and the consequent job-related despair and insecurity will make some turn to faith- or identity-based communities for solace or anchor or for alternative sources of pride, which are sometimes not very inclusive.

The populist demagogues in different parts of the world who have rallied communities for the cause of "taking back control," apart from being rabidly exclusivist, have, however, rarely devolved power to the local communities. While fulminating against supranational organizations and regulations, they have, if anything, centralized power at the national level. Paradoxically, in such attempts to strengthen the nation-state the right-wing populists are sometimes in the uncomfortable / unwitting company of state socialists and other antiglobalists on the Left; and ideologically pitted against them are the motley bunch of anarcho-communitarians, small-is-beautiful Gandhian thinkers, and Hayekian libertarians, as well as proglobal separatists (like those in Catalonia or Scotland).

3

The Wildfire of Resurgent Nationalism

Albert Einstein in an October 1929 interview with the *Saturday Evening Post* called nationalism "an infantile disease, the measles of mankind." Many contemporary cosmopolitan liberals are similarly skeptical, contemptuous, or dismissive, as its current epidemic rages all around the world, particularly in the form of right-wing extremist or populist movements. While one understands the liberal attitude, it would be irresponsible of us to let illiberal people hijack the idea of nationalism for their nefarious purpose. Nationalism is too passionate and historically explosive to be left to their tender mercies. It is important to fight the virulent forms of the disease with an appropriate antidote and try to vaccinate as many as possible, particularly in the younger generations. Or keeping the metaphor of fire, we may have to learn the methods of controlled burning that the fighters of forest fires often adopt.

Populists advocate a culturally narrow, narcissistic, nostalgic, and xenophobic form of ethnic nationalism—from the Christian nationalism of evangelicals in the United States, Catholic nationalists in Poland, or Orthodox Church followers' nationalism in Russia to Islamic nationalism in Indonesia and Turkey or Hindu nationalism in India. We are going to examine in this chapter an alternative, more inclusive, form of nationalism often counterposed to this as some variant of what is called civic nationalism.

THE HISTORICAL ORIGIN OF NATIONALISM

Let us start with a brief historical note. As a form of community bonding on the basis of some tribal or ethnic territorial connections, proton-ationalisms of various kinds have old and durable roots in different societies. Yet as Ernest Gellner, one of the foremost theorists of nation-alism, has pointed out, nationalism in the form as we know it is of relatively recent origin. Of course, historical memories and myths (my-thology is often blurred into historical facts and legends), symbols, and traditions are constantly invoked in the name of ethnic nationalism even though, as the distinguished historian Eric Hobsbawm famously points out in the Introduction to Hobsbawm and Ranger (2012), many of the so-called traditions are actually of recent invention. The influ-ential nineteenth-century French scholar Ernest Renan likewise pointed out, in a lecture at the Sorbonne in 1882, how "historical error" is used in the creation of a nation. Gellner even points to cases of nationalism based on not much history at all; in a debate at Warwick University in 1995 he said, "The Estonians created nationalism out of thin air in the course of the nineteenth century."

But what is often overlooked is that there is a clear distinction between nationalism based on some *social* bonding principle and the nation-*state* that became a predominant political unit, at least in Europe, after the 1648 Peace of Westphalia. The former refers to a sociological community based on some homogeneous binding element like religion, language, ethnicity or culture, whereas the latter is a political community that need not contain a singular sociological na-tionality. Yet the European idea of the nation-state, where sociological and political communities are congruent, has become the basis of our predominant idea about nationalism, and both Gellner and Hobsbawm essentially adhere to this idea. But what about multinational societies? Even in western Europe, Belgium, Spain, and Switzerland are examples of nation-states with diverse linguistic and sociological communities where the singular principle of national binding does not work.

Let us now take possibly the largest such multinational society in the world: India. Indian social thinkers made contributions to thoughts on nationalism in the context of intranational diversity more than a hundred years ago, and these have been underappreciated in Western theories of nationalism. I have particularly in mind Mahatma Gandhi and Rabindranath Tagore. Both expressed their ideas on nationalism in the first three decades of the twentieth century in various forms (essays and lectures by both and, in the case of Tagore, also in literature with several poems and at least three novels—one of which later was the basis of a widely known Satyajit Ray movie, *The Home and the World*). They were, of course, both anti-imperialists, thus sharing in the popular movements of nationalism against colonial rulers, but they wanted to go beyond this to think about a more positive basis of nationalism that could sustain the country when the colonial rulers left. Both of them found the nation-state of European history—with a singular social homogenizing principle, militarized borders, and jingoistic mobilization against supposed enemy states—unacceptable and unsuitable for India's diverse and heterogeneous society. They looked at the various groups who migrated into India throughout history, who in conjunction with the indigenous people, came to form an amorphous composite culture that in spite of the various particularistic linguistic and cultural imaginings of the nation in different parts of the country has some discernible pattern of unity in diversity. They both drew upon the long folk-syncretic tradition of Indian society—which grew out of the sedimentary layers formed by the successive waves of social reform and rebellion known collectively as the Bhakti movement, against the dominance of the rigid Hindu Brahminical system over many centuries in different regions of India, and out of the Sufi sects of Islam. It was a tradition that extolled interfaith tolerance and pluralism, and both Gandhi and Tagore wanted to make that the constructive basis of Indian nationalism.

Of course, respect for pluralism has not always been robust in the face of myriad sources of intercommunity tensions and conflicts in India. Even violence has not been uncommon from time to time. Of course, as Asghar Ali Engineer's 1984 book, *Communal Riots in Post-Independence India* meticulously documents, conflicts and violence were often stoked by vested interests motivated by various—often material—reasons, and they ultimately took on a communal color. For example, if real estate interests wanted to evict slum dwellers to make room for their lucrative development projects, and the majority of the slum's residents happened to be Muslim (or Hindu), they would hire Hindu (or Muslim) goons to start some ugly incidents, which would soon degenerate into violence between the two communities, often resulting in arson, eviction, and, ultimately, the clearing of the slum. The whole episode would later be branded in police documents as another case of a communal riot. Paul Brass, in his 2003 book *The Production of Hindu-Muslim Violence in Contemporary India,* cites many instances of how riots are "produced" by motivated agents as part of the political mobilization process. In spite of such episodic conflicts, the general atmosphere in much of India, at least until recently, has been one of intercommunity pluralism and tolerance (though not necessarily fraternity and harmony), and even participation in one another's cultural activities.

On the issue of the nation-state, as I mentioned earlier in Chapter 2, Gandhi, who had described himself as an "enlightened anarchist," was not favorably disposed to the modern state. Tagore was less averse to modernity in general, but he was trenchant in his criticism of the Western idea of the nation-state, "with all its paraphernalia of power and prosperity, its flags and pious hymns, . . . its mock thunders of patriotic bragging," and of how it stoked a national conceit that made society lose its moral balance. Jawaharlal Nehru, who was personally close to Gandhi but ideologically closer to Tagore, saw the modern state as essential for providing a unifying structure in a divided society and for unleashing the forces of planned economic development in a world of poverty and inequality.

CIVIC AS OPPOSED TO ETHNIC NATIONALISM

By the time the Constitution of India was framed in 1949 both Gandhi and Tagore were dead. Nehru (along with B. R. Ambedkar), following their lead, drew upon the society-centered and pluralistic idea of nationalism and gave it a legal-juridical form in the new constitution. The Nehru-Ambedkar idea of nationalism, forged and refined through the elaborate deliberations of the Constituent Assembly, gave India the basis of its civic nationalism, which more or less prevailed for many decades. It is not that such civic nationalism was firmly established immediately after the constitution started operation, but it achieved widespread legitimacy as an anchor of everyday civic practice and as a continuing public educational and aspirational goal. As Madhav Khosla mentions in *India's Founding Moment: The Constitution of a Most Surprising Democracy* (2020), the constitution for India's large diverse and fractured population was not just a rule book but also a textbook for continuing political education.

It is this inclusive idea of civic nationalism that Hindu nationalists are now attempting to dismantle as they privilege a unified Hindu nation-state that supersedes all particularistic divisions and subordinates and humiliates the non-Hindu minorities. Even at the time of the framing of the constitution, the Rashtriya Swayamsevak Sangh (RSS), their main ideological base organization, had opposed the constitution as "Western," even though in their own earlier history many of their leaders used to admire the ethnic basis of nationalism in Germany (their revered leaders, like Madhavrao Sadashivrao Golwalkar and Vinayak Damodar Savarkar, had expressed open admiration for the "efficient" Nazi system of mobilizing and organizing the German nation). Earlier the Japanese nation-state had also been inspired by German history. It is not surprising that Tagore's lectures in Japan as early as 1916 against the aggrandizing nation-state did not make him popular with many Japanese, who had originally been effusive about him (as Asia's first Nobel laureate). Much later, in 1938, shortly after the Japanese invasion of China, a Japanese poet and friend wrote to Tagore seeking moral support for Japan's action since China was being "saved" from the clutches of the West; Tagore was severely critical and described the Japanese poet's sentiments as translating "military swagger into spiritual bravado."

There are, of course, many routes to pluralism. A relative degree of tolerance for diversity and for minority rights had at times characterized some autocratic empire states in history (like Mughal or Ottoman). Among democratic nations, the United States was a pioneer in making pluralism and liberal constitutional values the basis of nationalism. After the decimation of the indigenous population, a country without much historical memory essentially became a nation of immigrants. Abraham Lincoln's Gettysburg Address starts by referring to the "nation, conceived in Liberty, and dedicated to the proposition that all men are created equal."

In 1973 Hannah Arendt, when asked about her dominant impression about the United States in an interview on French television, said, "This country is united neither by heritage, nor by memory, nor by soil, nor by language, nor by origin from the same . . . and these citizens are united only by one thing—and that is a lot. That is, you become a citizen of the United States by simple consent to the Constitution." In an April 6, 2009, speech Barack Obama said, "One of the great strengths of the United States is . . . we do not consider ourselves a Christian nation . . . we consider ourselves a nation of citizens who are bound by ideals and a set of values," presumably as enshrined in the US Constitution.

In spite of its many historical (and often racially motivated) lapses, this is a major example in history of what the German philosopher Jürgen Habermas calls "constitutional patriotism." This he opposes to the patriotism based on "blood and soil" that had popular appeal in Germany—and which appeals to today's populist nationalists, and which in history has been associated with a great deal of persecution, violence, and devastation. Habermas has even argued that immigrants to a liberal democratic state need not assimilate into the host culture but only accept the principles of the country's constitution. This means that multiculturalism is acceptable as long as it is compatible with basic human rights enshrined in a democratic constitution. So the more permissive kind of multiculturalism—where all groups are allowed their peculiar cultural practices, however repugnant they may be from the human rights point of view (by one mocking description, this amounts to "liberalism for the liberals, cannibalism for the cannibals")—is not acceptable under civic nationalism. This diffuses some of the usual complaints of ethnic nationalists against culturally alien immigrants.

Of course, the idea of civic nationalism is, as Yael Tamir (2019) has pointed out, often too abstract and legalistic and provides too thin a basis for political mobilization, particularly in countries where liberal institutions are weak. Various forces unleashed by economic and cultural insecurity can weaken the foundations of civic nationalism and there may be oscillations between forms of civic and ethnic nationalism. Tamir cites German history as an example of such oscillations: "Following the German epic trail from the Enlightenment to romanticism, nationalism, fascism, Nazism, and finally to a constitutional democracy and the current reemergence of (ethnic) nationalism teaches us an important lesson about the oscillation of nations from ethnic to civic realities and back." Comparing forty-four countries over two decades Christian Albrekt Larsen (2017) shows how countries vacillate between civic and ethnic versions (and degrees) of nationalism in response to social and political events and crises.

ETHNIC NATIONALISM IRONING OUT DIVERSITY

Our identities are necessarily multilayered, but ethnic nationalism privileges one (or a limited few) of these layers—usually based on the narrow particularities of religion, language, or culture—that makes it easy to mobilize certain groups. Liberal or folk-syncretic traditions are sometimes too fragile to resist our primordial or visceral evolutionary defensive-aggressive urge to fight against "enemy" groups that the ethnic nationalist leaders are adept at whipping up. The branded enemy groups are both external and internal. In China, Hungary, India, Indonesia, Poland, Russia, and elsewhere, the internal minority groups are often victims of suspicion by the majoritarian ethnic nationalists who portray them as the proverbial fifth column aiding an enemy state.

Even without an enemy state, nationalist leaders worry that the inevitable divisions of a heterogeneous society will undermine their homogenizing mission; hence, such nationalism is almost always associated with riding roughshod over the "little people" and their localized cultures for the larger cause of national integration. For this cause marginal groups like low-caste and indigenous people in India (e.g., Adivasis and Dalits) have to be crammed into the Procrustean fold of the larger Hindu society. Western Europe in the nineteenth century provides such examples too, as in the way the hitherto disparate and fragmented rural people of France, many of whom as late as 1863 did not speak French, but a diverse array of patois, were homogenized, schooled into the standardized French national language and identity in just a few decades, as narrated in the remarkable book by Eugen Weber, *Peasants into Frenchmen* (1976). Putin's revanchist nationalism forcibly trying to bring the Ukranians into the Russan fold is a more recent, more violent example from Eastern Europe.

In China, the ruthless Han sinification of Tibetans and Uighurs and the harsh suppression of even the feeblest expression of their cultural autonomy have been considered imperative for the cause of Chinese ethnic nationalism. China, of course, has a long history of homogenization of culture and language, and suppression of voices of dissent reflexively taken as signs of rebellion. The historian W. J. F. Jenner, in his book *The Tyranny of History* (1992), describes one of the basic tenets of Chinese civilization as "that uniformity is inherently desirable, that there should be only one empire, one culture, one script, one tradition."

In the name of national integration and fighting enemies both outside and within, ethnic nationalists undermine minority rights and the procedures of democracy (due process), accuse liberals of appeasing the minorities (blacks and Hispanics in the United States, immigrants in Europe, Kurds in Turkey, Muslims in India, etc.), and try to suppress dissent as "antinational." Civic nationalism, on the other hand, emphasizes the procedural aspects of democracy, and through its stress on liberal constitutional values tries to use the precommitment of a foundational document to bind the hands of subsequent generations if they display majoritarian tendencies that curb basic civil rights. During the civil rights movement Martin Luther King Jr. was referring to the US Constitution when he appealed to Americans "to be true to what you said on paper" in his final speech the night before he died.

One reason why ethnic nationalist populists are opposed to globalization is that they are against global rules restraining national sovereignty; they want to "take back control." But in so doing, as I noted at the end of the Chapter 2, they give too much power to the national leader, dissipate the forces of decentralization, and erode the autonomy of local communities. In contrast, civic nationalism often emphasizes local autonomy; that is why, for example, political parties like the Scottish National Party favor civic over ethnic nationalism (though, of course, Anglophobia is not totally absent among them).

Overcentralization in the name of national unity ultimately polarizes and weakens the nation, as diversity and autonomy get trampled upon. In large and diverse societies federalism acts as a safety valve for interregional tension, which may be activated by this overcentralization. Of course, the reaction varies also with the type of federalism, which depends on the political history of a country. Political analysts distinguish between *coming-together* federalism (as in the case of the United States) and *holding-together* federalism (as in the case of India). Unlike in the former, many of the residual and emergency powers are vested by the constitution in the federal government in *holding-together* federalism, with a near unitary structure as a default mode; this makes it easier to centralize in the name of national unity, particularly in the face of a perceived danger from an enemy state. We saw this in 2019 when the Hindu nationalist government of India robbed the Muslim-majority state of Jammu and Kashmir of its autonomy in the name of national security and broke it up into three centrally administered territories, something that would be nearly impossible to do in the United States.

ECONOMIC NATIONALISM

Let us now turn to the economic aspects of globalization, to which nationalists of the two types may respond differently. Ethnic nationalist populists tend to look at the global economy as a zero-sum game: gains for "them" is necessarily a loss for "us," harking back to a defunct mercantilist doctrine. By now it is obvious that a Trump-style trade war and the dismantling of multilateral trade rules do not quite advance the national agenda. (In Chapter 9 I will discuss how international coordination in mitigating climate change or the pandemic serves vital national interests.) In today's world economy of integrated global value chains and continuous swapping of parts, components, and tasks across borders, a retreat from relatively free trade will be extremely harmful for the national interests of most countries. Trade makes for cheaper producer inputs on which our production base is heavily dependent. It's also crucial for the cheaper mass consumer goods available from Amazon or Walmart, and for creating larger markets for the goods from developed countries now demanded by the rising middle classes in developing countries.

Economic nationalism has, of course, been associated with vigorous industrial policies in East Asia, with the state guiding and supporting some key domestic manufacturing industries (particularly in sectors where coordination failures of the market and "learning by doing" processes are important). In cases where the initial costs of entry are large and lumpy, and demand is uncertain, the state has a special role in priming the pump and encouraging new entry. But in the East Asian cases where industrial policy succeeded, one has to keep in mind that ultimately market discipline—mostly coming from open export markets and heightened cost consciousness and quality consciousness—made the all-important difference between success and failure. Philippe Aghion and colleagues (2015) cite panel data from medium and large Chinese enterprises from 1998 to 2007 to show that industrial policies targeted to competitive sectors or that foster competition (e.g., policies that are more dispersed across firms in a sector or that encourage younger and more productive enterprises in a sector) increase productivity growth.

Liberal nationalists should, of course, call for a substantial strengthening of the "adjustment assistance" to those hurt by globalization. Such assistance is paltry in the United States and nonexistent in many developing countries. Likewise, retraining programs should last for a long enough period to significantly improve the adjustment capability of workers in coping with trade shocks, and making benefits (like health care) portable rather than linked to particular jobs. In much of Europe, better safety nets and more active labor market policies than in the United States, especially for workers who lose their jobs, have made import penetration less of a burning issue in the political sphere.

Liberals are divided on the issue of unrestricted international capital flows and that of immigration. Given the adverse effects of free capital flows on periodic macroeconomic shocks and the weakening of the bargaining power of domestic labor institutions, many otherwise free-traders agree with the liberal nationalists on strengthening regulations on global capital flows (even the International Monetary Fund now seems to hesitantly concur in this), the so-called sand in the wheels of international finance. Of course, there is some disagreement on the desirable extent of such restrictions, and also on their practicability, after a point. Controls are easier to evade in a world of superconnectivity.

Some compromises are also possible on the need for adjusting global rules, giving nations more autonomy on labor standards. Civic nationalists also accept some restrictions on national sovereignty to agree on multilateral rules on global public goods, as in the case of global environmental damage or global public health (including monitoring and preventing pandemics), the international spread of crime or cyberattacks, and restrictions on cross-border tax-dodging, all of which ultimately help the national interest.

Given the cultural anxiety that large-scale immigration generates in many societies, there is also scope for compromise on various schemes to limit the flows of immigration—to selected areas where there are specific skill shortages in rich countries and to some special humanitarian cases. There are some constructive economic proposals for defusing some of the anti-immigrant tension. Take, for example, the Global Compact, a nonbinding international agreement endorsed by the General Assembly of the United Nations. In that context it has been proposed that rich countries will identify particular skill shortages at home—for example, certain kinds of nursing or caregiving services—and start funding training centers for such service workers located in poor countries. Only a controlled number of graduates of those centers will then be part of an immigration permit system, leaving others to serve needs at home. This way both the need to relieve specific skill shortages in rich countries (at a lower cost than training them in those countries) and the need to mitigate the impact of skills drain from poor countries are served. (One has to be, of course, careful that this does not reinforce underinvestment in vocational education and training for the local working class in rich countries.) One can think of many such global skill partnerships.

One set of compromise on immigration suggested by Branko Milanović in his recent book *Capitalism Alone* (2019) is the introduction of "citizenship lite," giving incremental access to welfare benefits and other social and economic rights for immigrants, ending the strictly binary division between citizens and noncitizens. This is intended to make immigration more palatable politically in rich countries while giving immigrants from poor countries only a part of the "rent" that a citizen from a rich country enjoys by having won the (country) lottery at birth. Of course, to a cosmopolitan social democrat this explicitly creates a category of second-class citizens and violates the democratic concept of citizenship and belonging. But any such compromise is for the second- or third-best world, with many constraints: social, economic and cultural. In any case, there currently exist different categories of visa for noncitizen immigrants, with different opportunities for ultimately obtaining full citizenship. The idea, one presumes, is to keep pushing the boundary of compromise as much as possible in favor of poor workers in the current anti-immigration climate.

One should also be careful in not exaggerating anti-immigration anxiety, even while it is palpably real among many. In a survey of twenty-two thousand citizens in twenty democracies in 2021 by YouGov and Global Progress (reported by Halpin in 2021), 58 percent of respondents said it was "very important" to have "clear, consistently applied rules about who can come to our country"; only 44 percent said "limiting numbers" was "very important." So immigration in a fair and controlled manner, without much rule-breaking, may be acceptable to the majority of people. The new coalition government in Germany has announced that it will reduce irregular immigration while enabling more regular immigration. Even ethnic citadels like Japan have now started showing a more relaxed attitude to permanent immigrants.

In general, populists invidiously distinguish between nationalists and globalists. This is highly misleading: not only are there other, more liberal, forms of nationalism, but also not all liberals are for untrammeled hyperglobalization. It is thus possible and necessary to build healthy alternatives to the kinds of rabid ethnic nationalism that we see all around us without giving up on the nationalist cultural pride or the bonding of local communities consistent with the democratic spirit and larger humanitarian principles. As Tagore said in his lectures on nationalism in Japan in 1916, "Neither the colorless vagueness of cosmopolitanism, nor the fierce self-idolatry of nation-worship, is the goal of human history."

4

The Temptation of Authoritarianism

These days there seems to be a growing consensus—as enunciated, for example, in Branko Milanović's 2019 book *Capitalism Alone*—that capitalism is more or less the only viable socioeconomic system left in the world, but that there are substantially different types of political organization of the capitalist system. The two types that attract prime attention are liberal democratic capitalism, as broadly prevailing in many Western countries, subject to some cases of populist distortions; and authoritarian capitalism under the guidance of a meritocratic state, of which China is the glitteringly successful recent example. We shall examine in Chapter 7 the alternative model of social democracy, which features some important modifications of capitalism to help the system resist populist distortions and strengthen worker control without giving up either on liberal democracy or the incentives to innovate. In this chapter I analyze the general ingredients of a strong effective state that is often recommended for the execution of public policy and, in this context and in some detail, the challenge of the Chinese model—particularly the strengths and weaknesses of its governance features.

THE CHINA DEVELOPMENT MODEL

Today China and its "wolf warrior" diplomats lose no opportunity to trumpet the success story of the China model. Their leaders have long forsaken Deng Xiaoping's advice to keep a low profile (*tao guang yang hui*). In declaring a new era for China during the Nineteenth National Congress in Beijing in 2017, President Xi Jinping presented the Chinese system of governance as a model for other countries to emulate. Leaders who "want to speed up their development while preserving their independence," Xi said, should look to China as "a new option." Many people, in both rich and poor countries, seem already to be awestruck by this model.

What are the special characteristics of the Chinese development model? Briefly, it's a model of essentially capitalist development under authoritarian leadership and purposive governance. It features a vertical production structure in which basic capital goods are produced by state-owned monopolies while the (much larger) remainder of the economy is under private ownership. It is guided by a state-led nationalist industrial policy and finance system, with subsidized access to land and credit for state-favored business, repression of labor rights, and massive investments in infrastructure funded by a very high national savings rate (particularly on account of large undistributed profits from companies), with a focus on rural industrialization in a decentralized framework of jurisdictional competition, openness to foreign trade and acquisition and learning of foreign technology, and (more recently) concentration on the development of new technology in selected sectors. It has produced a rapid pace of economic growth over the past three decades and lifted several hundreds of millions of people above the poverty line, eliminating most of extreme poverty—undoubtedly a spectacular historic feat for any developing country. The slowing of the growth rate in recent years does not tarnish this shining performance over the long term.

The model seems to have gotten a further boost during the COVID-19 pandemic. Even though the pandemic started in Wuhan, China, the government took control of the situation after some initial fumbling and obfuscation, and with massive efforts at mobilization and surveillance largely controlled the spread of the disease and its subsequent resurgence (though the official data on total infection and death rates are dubious and the current emphasis on zero infection seems like going overboard). Chinese propaganda even claimed that the nation's success shows how an authoritarian system is better at controlling pandemics compared to some of the flailing democracies. Of course, it deliberately ignored the reasonably successful examples of control of the pandemic in democratic countries like Austria, Costa Rica, Denmark, Germany, New Zealand, and Uruguay, and, in China's immediate neighborhood, Japan, South Korea, and Taiwan. (In the subsequent waves of the pandemic and in the vaccine rollout, some of the latter countries faltered, but so did China.)

DEMOCRACY AND DEVELOPMENT

Before we weigh the general claims about the Chinese model, let us first briefly consider the large literature on democracy and development; we want to wade into only a small part of it here—particularly the part that is relevant to the problem of trade-offs between the political centralization of power and the accountability to people. The relationship between democracy or pluralism (politically "inclusive" institutions in general) and development is actually rather complex, and the complexity is not captured in the usual international statistical regressions in the literature that link the development or growth performance of countries with some measure of each nation's ranking on the Democracy Index. The relation between democracy and growth in these regressions is not usually robust, strategies used to identify the relation are often not credible, and different papers in the literature have different results because of different choices of control variables and other forms of model uncertainty. For our present purpose, however, what is more important is that the statistical regressions do not help us understand the mechanism in the complex process involved.

Authoritarian leaders have an advantage over their democratic peers in situations that require quick decisions; democracy is, of course, excruciatingly slow. But its deliberative and electoral processes manage social conflicts better and lend some stabilizing legitimacy to policy decisions that grow out of the conditional consent of citizens. In addition, as Amartya Sen emphasized in his 1999 book *Development as Freedom*, democracy enriches individual autonomy and freedom, participation, and deliberation, which may be regarded as an important part of the process of human development itself. The abuses of human rights that are routine in authoritarian countries make the quality of development much poorer, however dazzling the growth rate may be.

A properly functioning democracy also tends to curb the excesses of capitalism and thus render development more sustainable—by, for example, encouraging social movements as watchdogs against environmental despoliation. To the autocrat, power is too valuable to lose, and hence violence and the attendant potential shattering of economic stability and the social fabric are never very far off. Autocratic regimes have also shown a larger variability in economic performance than have democratic states, as the checks and balances in the latter are supposed to weed out some of the worst leaders and outcomes. In comparison, one may be stuck with a bad autocrat for too long a time; history is littered with instances of incompetent but durable tyranny.

On the other hand, there are many cases of electoral democracies functioning without regular or fully operational institutionalized procedures of accountability. Even in liberal democracies, accountability processes to the general public are seriously undermined by the influence of money in lobbying for protecting and promoting the interests of the wealthy and powerful and in financing election of candidates who secure those interests. Even more generally, inequality in education, network building, and job credentialing, accumulated over generations, can perpetuate a form of "hereditary meritocracy" that renders liberal democracy a sham.

In addition, while political competition is usually assumed to be a good thing, analogous to market competition, there are cases in which competition can lead to a race to the bottom. Without political centralization, political competition under democracy can encourage competitive short-termism: come election time, Indian politicians, for example, often promise free electricity and water, which can wreck the prospects of long-term investments in the relevant infrastructure, or bank loan waivers for farmers, which can wreck the banking system. Many scarce resources are thus frittered away in short-term subsidies and handouts, which hurt the cause of long-term pro-poor investments (e.g., in roads, irrigation, drinking water, and electricity). Robert Bates (2008) gives examples from Africa of how competitive democracy could induce the ruling party to use its power to loot the public resources for short-term gain.

Of course, in the delivery of social services, political competition can work better when executive action is easily verifiable (it is, for example, easier to verify the lowering of school fees than the improvement of school quality). Consistent with this, Robin Harding and David Stasavage (2012) cite evidence that, in Africa, democracies have higher rates of school attendance than do nondemocracies. Similarly, there is evidence in Brazil that the political participation of the poor and the illiterate resulted in greater health spending and improved child health outcomes, and that in many African countries infant mortality fell significantly after democratization.

In some cases, instead of providing broad-based public goods, political leaders can work out a clientelistic system for dispensing selective benefits (private or club goods) to at least a group of swing voters to win elections. For example, in my own work with Dilip Mookherjee (Bardhan and Mookherjee 2020), in rural West Bengal we find evidence that voting behavior is significantly influenced more by recurring benefits arranged by local governments, and thus continual dependence on them (like subsidized credit or agricultural inputs, employment on public works, or help in personal emergencies), than by even large one-time benefits (like land reforms or provision of houses and latrines), suggesting political clientelism. Additionally, in situations of social and ethnic heterogeneity, where the mobilization of votes gets organized on sectarian lines, there may be more selective distribution of patronage and less political interest in investing in general-purpose public goods, as suggested by a field experiment that Leonard Wantchekon (2003) conducted in Benin. Such political clientelism, even while helping some poor people, can harm the cause of general pro-poor public investments. Thomas Fujiwara and Wantchekon (2013) cite some experimental evidence from Benin that shows how informed public deliberation in town hall meetings can reduce clientelism.

THE NATURE OF A STRONG STATE

In carrying out development programs or in handling a crisis of insecurity (e.g., of public health or the macroeconomy), what is often needed is an effective and well-coordinated state. Authoritarianism (or democracy) is neither necessary nor sufficient for this. There have been many authoritarian countries (e.g., in Africa or Latin America) that have failed miserably in such situations, while there have been democratic countries (Denmark, Germany, Japan, New Zealand, South Korea, and Sweden) that have been reasonably successful. One often hears the pat prescription that one needs a "strong" state, which, of course, need not be an authoritarian state. But how do you then define state strength? The strength of a state in this context has, of course, to be defined in a noncircular way (without reference to the performance outcome). A search of the literature suggests two somewhat overlapping components of a definition of state strength: (1) political centralization, and (2) the government's capacity to credibly commit.

Political centralization refers to the ability of the state to establish a cohesive order across local jurisdictions. It can then take into account the spillover effects of policy actions of different local authorities, enabling an encompassing organization to override various local particularistic and divergent pressures. Such centralization also provides incentives for incumbent political leaders to invest in the creation of fiscal and legal capacity, as suggested by Timothy Besley and Torsten Persson (2011). Philip Osafo-Kwaako and James Robinson (2013) cite evidence from a cross-cultural sample for a strong positive correlation between political centralization (defined as "jurisdictional hierarchy beyond local community") and different measures of public goods and development outcomes. For eleven European countries, over four centuries, Mark Dincecco and Gabriel Katz (2016) show a direct positive relation between fiscal centralization and economic growth. For different African polities, Sanghamitra Bandyopadhyay and Elliot Green (2012) and Stelios Michalopoulos and Elias Papaioannon (2013) similarly provide direct econometric evidence of the positive impact of historical measures of political centralization on contemporary economic development.

A more general characteristic of a strong and effective state is the capacity to make credible commitments in the face of pressures from diverse interest groups. An important example of the strong state's ability to precommit arises in the case of the popular infant-industry argument for protection (i.e., the idea that protection is needed when an industry is in an early stage of development). In the past two hundred years this argument has been applied by the state in many countries in the early stages of industrialization, with a few successes and numerous failures, which has partly to do with the strength of the state or the lack of it. At the time when such protection is initiated, by the very nature of this argument it is meant to be for a short period until the industry infant stands up on its own two feet. But in most countries infant-industry protection inevitably faces the time inconsistency problem: when the initial period of protection nears its completion, the political pressures for its renewal from vested interests become inexorable, and in this way the infant industry in a weak state can degenerate into a geriatric protection lobby (the history of import-substituting industrialization in developing countries is full of such examples).

In the recent history of the strong states of East Asia, however, there have been some remarkable instances of the government keeping its commitment, withdrawing protection from an industry if it does not shape up after the lapse of a preannounced duration and letting the industry sink or swim in international competition; Robert Wade (1990) gives some examples of this.

A closely related commitment issue is that of enforcing a hard budget constraint in projects run or funded by the public sector. A strong state should be better at resisting the inevitable bailout pressures from interests involved in failing projects. A weak state is unable to make a credible commitment to terminate a bad public project.

Another important aspect of the quality of state intervention in recent East Asian history has to do with the use, by and large, of clear, well-defined, preannounced rules of performance criteria. In South Korea, for example, the heavy involvement of the state in directing investment through subsidized credit allocation has been largely successful because of its strict adherence to the criterion of export performance. Through this precommitment device the strong Korean state has used the vital disciplining function of foreign competition in encouraging quick learning, cost consciousness, and quality consciousness among domestic enterprises, something that has been conspicuously absent in many other interventionist regimes (even though the Korean state at least until the 1980s shared with the latter regimes many of the restrictive policies on imports and foreign investment). Of course, some East Asian states were authoritarian in their early development stage (even though South Korea and Taiwan later transited to democracy), but the history of democratic states like Germany, Japan, or Sweden also have many such instances of commitment.

THE INGREDIENTS OF STATE CAPACITY

Besley and Persson (2011) associate a weak state with a lack of state capacity—particularly fiscal, legal, and military capacity—to be able to provide public goods and services (including law and order). In the burgeoning literature on state capacity, different writers have emphasized different aspects. A well-known line of thinking associated with Charles Tilly (1985) links the historical making of the fiscal-military state in early modern Europe with interstate wars (or threats thereof). Margaret Levi (1988) associates state making with inducing citizens to comply in providing revenue and conscripts for war. Others, however, have suggested that in more recent times, and outside Europe, states have been formed without wars and that there have been cases where wars have unraveled preexisting states.

In examining the components of state capacity, Peter Evans and James Rauch (1999) stress the importance of certain Weberian characteristics of the state bureaucracy, like meritocratic recruitment and long-term career rewards for officials. There is also a cumulative logic of bureaucratic functioning. A long history of continuous bureaucratic structure in place may foster a helpful bureaucratic culture or esprit de corps that can contribute to state effectiveness. Valerie Bockstette, Areendam Chanda, and Louis Putterman (2002) have computed an index of state antiquity (measuring the extent of continuous territory-wide state structure that prevailed over local tribal domains over the last two millennia). It shows that among developing countries this index is much lower for Latin America and sub-Saharan Africa than for Asia, and even in Asia the index for Korea is several times that for the Philippines (a country that lacked an encompassing state before its sixteenth century colonization by Spain).

Jorge Cornick (2013) has classified the different types of state capacity into the *technical*, *organizational*, and *political*. Technical capacity is particularly relevant, for example, in the context of screening worthwhile public projects or monitoring the delivery to intended beneficiaries in social programs; information technology has expanded the realm of possibilities here. Karthik Muralidharan, Paul Niehaus, and Sandip Sukhtankar (2014) have evaluated the impact of a biometrically authenticated payments infrastructure on public employment and pension programs in India using a large-scale experiment that randomized the rollout of the new system over 158 subdistricts and nineteen million people. They find that the new system delivered a faster, more predictable, and less corrupt payments process without adversely affecting access to the program. These results suggest that investing in secure authentication and payments infrastructure can significantly add to state capacity in effective implementation of social programs in developing countries. Similar issues arise in the context of building capacities in judicial, auditing, and regulatory bodies.

The organizational capacity of a state is often crudely measured in the empirical literature in terms of tax to gross domestic product (GDP) ratio (with a higher ratio indicating a higher fiscal capacity of the state to carry out different projects). But, as is usually recognized, this ratio may be relatively high in a country abundant in natural resources on account of the resource rents, and not necessarily because of organizational capacity, or low in a poor country where for independent reasons (e.g., the nature of factor market imperfections) the informal sector is large. Organizational capacity is also related to modes of governance. For example, Oriana Bandiera, Andrea Prat, and Tomasso Valletti (2009) show, from a policy experiment associated with a national procurement agency in Italy, that much of the sheer wastage in public procurement arises from the way the relevant bodies are organized (with "top-down" governance modes in public bodies performing the worst).

Organizational capacity, of course, varies between different types of state functions. The Indian state has shown an extraordinary capacity in some large episodic events—like organizing the complex logistics of the world's largest elections for nine hundred million voters, for some of the world's largest religious festivals, or for the world's second largest census, or installing the world's largest biometric ID system for more than a billion people in just a few years. But the demands on state capacity from organizing temporary large events, mobilizing resources, or managing logistics are different from sustaining or institutionalizing the state's efforts, particularly at the local last-mile delivery of routine services on a continuing basis. The Indian state displays poor capacity in, for example, some regular and essential activities like the cost-effective pricing and distribution of electricity. This is partly because local political considerations interfere in matters like recovery of costs from a large and politically sensitive customer base.

As I have noted, political capacity is often largely an issue of commitment and resisting pressures for short-termism and soft budget constraints. In many parts of Africa and India the police and bureaucracy are highly politicized and deliberately incapacitated so that they serve the short-term political goals of leaders. In such contexts, measures to improve bureaucratic autonomy may enhance performance. In a study of forty-seven hundred public-sector projects implemented by the Nigerian Civil Service, Imran Rasul and Daniel Rogger (2018) find that an increase in autonomy for bureaucrats corresponds to significantly higher project completion rates.

In general, political capacity depends on the ability to form "social pacts" among important political stakeholders, the nature of political coalitions, and the distribution of power. In the early decades of its development, South Korea's political coalition involved a tight integration between a military bureaucracy and conglomerate business that was clearly out of bounds for the elite to accomplish in democratic India. But within India's democratic framework the relative weakness of state capacity has been more a symptom of the underlying political difficulty of organizing collective action for the long term (even among its divided elite), but not because the country lacks administratively capable people. Consistent with the theory of collective action, India's large heterogeneous population, fragmented polity, and high social and economic inequality make it hard to agree on long-term common goals and, even when such agreement is achieved, to get its act together in pursuit of those goals.

Almost by definition, divided societies and polities will have weaker common interests, and as Besley and Persson (2011) have pointed out, the incentive to invest in state capacity in such places will be lower. In contrast, in the postwar decades in Northeast Asia and northwest (particularly Nordic) Europe, relative social homogeneity and less unequal distribution of wealth and human capital may have made it somewhat less difficult to enlist the support of most social groups in making short-term sacrifices and coordinating growth-promoting policies. This reinforces the idea that the strength of the state is ultimately sustained by its breadth of support in the general population.

Self-sacrifice for the general and long-term good is obviously more likely if, as some cultural theorists point out, the predominant culture is *collectivist* (that is, when individuals internalize group interests through social norms), which is prominent in some description of East Asian societies, as opposed to *individualist*. This became particularly apparent recently in public attitudes to state guidelines on coping with the COVID-19 virus. Wearing masks and social distancing were much more easily accepted and adopted in East Asian societies than in the more individualistic and libertarian parts of Western societies.

An important but complicated question relating to the prevailing political coalition, and hence the political capacity of the state, that is seldom discussed in this context is its link with globalization, even leaving aside the usual constraints on state power in a global economy posed by volatile capital flows and international credit ratings. On the one hand, international competition and integration may strengthen domestic political accountability processes and make political coalitions somewhat more broad-based. Historically, for example, as Daron Acemoglu, Simon Johnson, and James Robinson (2005) show, the rise of international trade in the Atlantic economies during the early modern period promoted a demand for institutional reforms. In more recent times, European economic integration has been reported to have improved some governance institutions on Europe's southern and eastern peripheries. On the other hand, much depends on the initial conditions, the type of goods that are internationally traded, and the nature of political and economic competition. In many historical cases, expansion of trade in natural resources or products heavily dependent on them (like oil, sugar, bananas, timber, or diamonds) strengthened the political power of plantation elites and other large exporters who raised domestic barriers to entry and promoted oligarchic dominance over the state. More recently, globalization, in a context where capital is much more internationally mobile than labor, has weakened labor organizations and practices in many countries and altered the political equilibrium in favor of capital. The fall in customs revenue and capital taxes in a more open economy may also affect the state's fiscal capacity.

THE CHINESE GOVERNANCE SYSTEM: STRENGTHS AND WEAKNESSES

Now, after the general discussion of the meaning and possible ingredients of a strong state, we can put in perspective the strengths and weaknesses of China's system of governance. The governance system is an essential part of the so-called China development model. Yet it is less frequently discussed than other aspects of the model, and when it is discussed in the general literature on comparative governance, commentators outside China tend to focus on the simplistic distinction between authoritarianism and democracy. As I have briefly discussed elsewhere (Bardhan 2013), authoritarianism is neither necessary nor sufficient for some of the distinctive features of Chinese governance, both positive and negative—their roots actually go far back in history—just as various recent dysfunctions of governance in India and the United States are not inherent in their democratic processes.

I shall focus here on the following three aspects of Chinese governance, from the point of view of economic development, and occasionally draw comparison with governance features in India, the second largest developing country: (1) the internal organization of government; (2) the abuse of governance and corruption; and (3) decentralized structures and practices.

THE INTERNAL ORGANIZATION OF GOVERNMENT

Political Meritocracy

It is often pointed out that, unlike in most authoritarian countries, China has a political meritocracy. China's dramatic economic success has now convinced even some Western scholars (see, for example, the 2016 book by Daniel Bell, *The China Model: Political Meritocracy and the Limits of Democracy*), not to mention the members of the Chinese elite, that China's political meritocracy can perform as well as (or even better than) a multiparty democracy. This is an issue of special urgency at a time when there is widespread weakening of confidence in liberal democracy.

Officials in China are not merely selected on the basis of an examination system that goes way back in imperial history; their promotion also depends on how well the local economy performs. This approach to career development works better than that in, for example, democratic India's top administrative system, where promotion is based more on seniority than on performance, even though recruitment is similarly on the basis of civil service examinations.

An immediate question arises, however: Who in the political system defines what is meritorious and what is not?

It is possible that what may look like meritorious performance to the Chinese Communist Party (CCP) elite and its Central Organization Department, Zhongzubu, may not be considered so by many others in the general population, particularly in a large country with inevitable diversities and conflicts of objectives. This is not to speak of outlying regions, where the performance of centrally appointed provincial leaders considered meritorious by the party may not be judged so by many in the ethnic groups like Tibetans or Uighurs.

In general, how do we know what people consider as meritorious without institutions of downward accountability?

One of the distinctive features of democracy is that the criteria for meritorious performance arise out of open public discussion. Thus the assessment of a regime's performance may include considerations of pluralism and inclusiveness in the decision-making process itself. The judgment of democratic performance emphasizes the process as much as the outcome. In this process, citizens in a democracy are not treated as children; what is good for them is not decided by a patrimonial leadership, as is the case much too often in China (or Singapore). This is valid even when the leadership is very wise and benevolent.

In a democracy the performance criteria are also much more multifaceted, reflecting the pluralist agenda. It would be uncommon to reward an official mainly on the basis of the growth rate of the local economy. Of course, with many factors the incentives get diluted and are less effective. This seems to be happening now even in China, where other criteria (like environmental goals) are entering performance evaluation.

Performance versus Loyalty

The general understanding in China is that the career concerns of top officials act as key determinants of economic growth at the local level, and particularly the county and prefecture levels. And job rotation of officials at these levels provides useful on-the-job training at diverse localities. Of course, performance incentives can also generate plenty of side income or rent-earning opportunities. Officials, for example, might push for the sales of local government land and mining rights, which, while boosting local revenue and local development, can also be used to enable private illicit income for officials.

What about the large numbers of the rank-and-file public employees lower down the scale, who mostly remain in one place and for whom career incentives through promotion are not that relevant? They used to help themselves to all kinds of supplemental compensations, perks and benefits making up for low salaries. In other authoritarian countries, such systems of supplemental compensation sometimes degenerate into local loot and plunder—the proverbial extreme case is that of Zaire under President Mobutu Sese Seko, where soldiers and bureaucrats were not paid but left to fend for themselves (this tradition largely continues in the Democratic Republic of Congo even today). But in China it seems this system for the low-level officials was constrained from being excessive by the career concerns of the top local leaders dependent on the overall performance of the local economy.

A less well-known factor about Chinese promotion system is that as one climbs up the political ladder, to the provincial levels and beyond, the performance factor seems to diminish in importance in determining career prospects and the factor of political connections assumes greater significance. This is suggested, for example, by Pierre Landry, Xiaobo Lü, and Haiyan Duan (2017) in their analysis of a comprehensive data set of Chinese political appointments at the provincial, prefectural, and county levels. They find that the link between economic performance—in terms of GDP and revenue growth—and promotion is the strongest for county officials, significant for municipal officials, and insignificant for provincial officials. Similarly, from a comprehensive biographical database of all provincial leaders from 1978 until 2012 and an analysis of their promotion patterns, Fubing Su and Ran Tao (2016) find no evidence supporting the claim that competence played much of a role in central personnel decisions. Instead links with Politburo members and family connection with senior party leaders are more important.

There are also quid pro quo transactions. Using data for over a million land transactions during 2004–2016, Ting Chen and James Kai-sing Kung (2018) have shown that provincial party secretaries in selling local government land gave firms linked with Politburo members nearly 60 percent price discounts compared to others (and an even more substantial discount to the firms of members of the Politburo Standing Committee); in return, those who gave such discounts were estimated to be 23 percent more likely to be promoted to positions of national leadership (and, in general, the larger the discount, the higher the chance of promotion). Recent crackdowns, however, have somewhat reduced the chances for such promotions.

In any case, this general system of promotion has at least one important and beneficial implication: since performance incentives operate at least at the lower levels, higher-level leaders, even when they are selected on the basis of their loyalty to the current leadership at the top, are likely to have some measure of field-tested competence and experience.

This balance of performance and loyalty in determining an official's career path gives China a major advantage in the quality of its bureaucracy, compared to many other countries, including India and the United States, not to speak of many authoritarian countries where loyalty rules over minimum competence.

Of course, this also means that competent officials who are not sufficiently well connected to the top current leadership in China may reach a "glass ceiling." Some of them may then turn to alternative ways of earning rewards (including some corrupt ways), though these have been substantially curbed by recent anticorruption campaigns. There is even some evidence that high performers connected to previous top leaderships were particularly likely to be investigated, though the campaigns have gone much beyond merely penalizing rival power groups.

At this point, a comparison with other countries on ways of ensuring officials' loyalty to politicians may be interesting to note here. In India meritocratically recruited bureaucrats are manipulatively transferred. The threat of transfer to unattractive departments or locations acts to ensure loyalty to their political masters. The lure of plum postretirement jobs for ex-bureaucrats assigned by political leaders also work to keep the former pliant. All of this often means that junior officers underinvest in acquiring expertise, and one hears about corrupt deals between Indian politicians and bureaucrats in the process of "transfers and postings." There are similar stories about corrupt transactions in the buying and selling of positions in the Chinese bureaucracy, some of which have been revealed in the recent anticorruption campaigns. One finds from the data a vertical correlation between corruption indictments at higher and lower levels across provinces. In India such corruption may be somewhat more subject to public scrutiny from the media, social movements, and investigative agencies, which are usually more open and intensive than in China (although the misuse of the agencies by top leadership against political opponents has been rising in India and large parts of the media have become more docile).

In the United Kingdom manipulative transfers of officials are less common. In the United States, on the other hand, political loyalty is promoted by the unusually high turnover of senior civil servants (long before the announcement of a firing via Twitter became common under a recent president).

The political-bureaucratic distinction, particularly at higher levels, is, of course, blurred in China, as the party is supreme. But even in

Western democracies political control over senior appointments and promotions in public service has increased over time. Even in the United Kingdom, the insulation of career civil servants has declined somewhat, and this insulation has always been much weaker in the United States than in the United Kingdom (or Denmark or New Zealand).

The issue of political control pertains not just to the civil service but also to the various regulatory bodies that any complex economy requires, such as the entities that regulate public utilities (e.g., electricity, civil aviation, and telecommunications) and apex bodies regulating monetary or environmental policy or financial markets. Decisions in such regulatory bodies need special expertise and some insulation and independence from day-to-day political pressures and interference. Such independence is often completely lacking in the Chinese system; commitment to independence even when earnestly announced by the political leadership is not ultimately credible.

But even in democracies the balance between autonomous experts and the need for the periodic public review of their decisions to ensure accountability has been difficult to achieve. In India there are very few genuinely independent regulatory bodies (even apart from the problem of their capture by generalist Indian Administrative Service officers). Even the semi-independence of the Reserve Bank of India has been under some stress.

Organizational Capacity to Foster Technological Innovations

In the governance capacity to foster technological innovations, China has advanced much more than most developing countries. We see this particularly in the percentage of GDP devoted to research and development (R&D), though public support for R&D often neglects small- and medium-size enterprises); in the restructuring and upgrading of elite universities; and in various measures of progress in science and technology.

China, of course, has been very successful in the "catching-up" process of development, in learning and imitating off-the-shelf technology (sometimes making foreign partners in joint ventures part with their technology as a condition of access to its large market). In some day-to-day applications and enhancements of existing internet-based technology (e.g., in mobile payment, e-commerce, and transportation) China is now more advanced than the United States. China in general has been successful in what is called second-generation innovations (using established technologies to find new products and processes_ and much less so in cutting-edge technology. But even in the latter China is advancing, and it is currently engaging in a major technological race with the West in "deep tech" areas like artificial intelligence, quantum computing, chip making, biotechnology, and hypersonic military technology. (In this race the Chinese advances so far have not yet matched the huge amounts of government subsidies, investments, and procurement support.)

But in any future advances beyond the existing technological frontier China has both a major advantage and a major disadvantage. The advantage follows from the large size of the population and of the domestic market. Innovations, like those involving artificial intelligence and machine learning, that thrive on economies of scale, network externalities, and big data feedback loops will find hospitable ground in China.

The disadvantage follows from the lack of an open system that could encourage free spirit, critical thinking, challenges to incumbent organizations and methods, and diversity rather than conformity; these are necessary ingredients of many types of creative innovations. The current system of state promotion and guidance of globally successful large private technological enterprises is worth examining from this point of view. On the one hand, the state wants them to be "national champions"; on the other hand, it does not want them to be too internationally prominent or too financially successful—in particular, autonomously powerful enough to be outside the ambit of its control, supervision, and surveillance. In fact, over the last two decades state control with some financial investment in private companies, particularly in the tech sector, has increased significantly.

Will an autonomously successful firm be considered too "independent" for the comfort of the CCP? This was most recently evident in the way the government clamped down on the companies of one its most successful entrepreneurs, Jack Ma, after he gave a speech in October 2020 in which he was perceived by the top leadership to be (mildly) critical of some of the practices of state banks and regulators. The government dramatically stopped the initial public offering (which would have been the world's largest) of Ma's fintech company, Ant, and initiated an antitrust probe of Alibaba, his e-commerce giant. All of this happened in spite of the fact that these companies are central to China's online economy and Ma is a member of the party. Since then, other successful "platform" companies (like Didi and Tencent) and education technology companies have faced regulatory wrath. This has caused a great deal of uncertainty for private technology developers (particularly in the area of consumer services), as they'll always be wary of making what the party may consider political mistakes.

While all of this may be about the political price of too much success, there are also questions about failures. For example, will the Chinese state allow the full forces of "creative destruction" that Joseph Schumpeter (1942) has associated with innovations? In 2017 the total number of annual insolvency cases was smaller in China than even Romania, not to speak of the advanced industrial countries. More recently, some local companies in sectors like coal and property development have been allowed to default in the bond market, but whether groups controlled particularly by the central government will be allowed to face collapse is yet to be seen. The restructuring of the bankrupt gigantic property development company Evergrande, currently in process, with fallout throughout much of the economy, is being nervously watched by many.

Are today's successful incumbent firms—private or public—"too big to fail," or, in the case of clusters, "too many to fail"? Will the all-powerful CCP consider a major commercial failure or a prolonged stock market slump as a sign of lack of public confidence in it? Will it allow the development of independent legal institutions that are essential for an increasingly complex economy?

Much also depends on the nature of future innovations. Some innovations are of the *disruptive* kind that challenge incumbent firms—the US private innovators in collaboration with venture capitalists are good at this, and a politically connected, large, entrenched organization usually is not. Other innovations are of the steady *incremental* kind that adds up to significant gains (the Japanese call it *kaizen*); some large organizations in Germany, Japan, and South Korea have excelled in this. It is likely that the Chinese system is more conducive to this incremental kind of innovations.

Upward versus Downward Accountability

Even though at the top level of China's political system there is some degree of reciprocal accountability between the provincial and the central leadership, as provincial officials constitute about half of the Central Committee of the CCP that elects Politburo members, it is probably correct to say that the Chinese system is by and large one of upward accountability.

As I have noted, downward or democratic accountability provides governments with more political legitimacy, but can sometimes degenerate into pandering to short-term interests and pressure groups, particularly at election time. Short-term cyclical official behavior before the National People's Congress of the CCP is not unknown in China, but in general it is much easier for leaders to make long-term decisions under the Chinese governance system.

But a severe flaw of the upwardly accountable Chinese system is that mistakes in top-level decisions or outright abuses of power (in collaboration with crony business interests) take longer to detect and to correct, as the flow of information upward is tortuous or choked and the tendency to cover up is often too strong. Systems of upward accountability also face difficulty in inspiring bottom-up energies and spontaneous creativity. The recent abolition of term limits for the president and the decline of the collective leadership that Deng Xiaoping had put in place will make these problems more acute.

In multiparty democracies the open and adversarial relationships among the government, opposition parties, and the free media usually uncover mistakes and abuses much sooner than do authoritarian institutions. Corrections are prompted by public protests, agitations, and, ultimately, electoral sanctions. The information problem that even well-meaning bureaucrats in the Chinese system face is less severe in multiparty democracies. Of course, in China, unlike in many authoritarian countries, the information problem is partly relieved through decentralization.

Systemic Stability

Another serious question for Chinese governance concerns its mechanism for broad systemic self-correction. If the system is pushed off equilibrium by various kinds of political or economic shocks, how is it restored to equilibrium? In the face of a crisis the Chinese state often tends to overreact, suppress information, and act heavy-handedly, thereby sometimes magnifying the dimensions of the crisis. Even in the initial fumbling over the outbreak of the COVID-19 pandemic in Wuhan—the same thing had happened during the SARS outbreak—the lower-level officials had an incentive to suppress bad news. This systemic feature also generates a low tolerance for short-term economic volatility and the rush to reckless fiscal policies that exacerbate the staggering problems of capital misallocation that China faces. The institutional mechanisms for structural reform have now become particularly weaker, as the resolution of internal governance conflicts is now more dependent on personalized channels.

There also remains the larger institutional issue that China has faced throughout history: how to institutionally guarantee the rule of a "good emperor," as opposed to a bad one, or to ensure that a good emperor does not turn bad. The recent disruption in the conventions of collective leadership and the acceleration of the cult of personality in leadership can only worsen this problem.

As the economy becomes more complex and social relations become more convoluted and intense, the absence of transparent and accountable processes and the attempts by a "control freak" leadership to force lockstep conformity and discipline will generate acute tension, conflicts, and informational inefficiency.

In India, despite all the recent ominous signs of a democracy sliding into a form of a majoritarian overreach, it is probably still correct to say that the system structurally remains somewhat more resilient than in China. But in both countries (more in China than in India) nationalist glory and the cult of personality surrounding the top leader are becoming a convenient cover for any lapse in performance.

THE ABUSE OF GOVERNANCE AND CORRUPTION

Over the last quarter century there has been a tight, often collusive, relationship between business and politicians in China. This is evident from (1) frequent interchanges of positions between executives in public-sector companies and the party's Central Committee; (2) the fact that some of China's richest private businessmen are members of the

National People's Congress and the People's Political Consultative Conference, an important advisory body (there are even accounts of large "donations" made before such businessmen are selected for these bodies in China); and (3) the number of influential party members who can be described as plutocrats—the wealth data from Hurun's "China Rich List 2020" suggest that the average net worth of the richest seventy members of the National People's Congress in China is several times that for the richest seventy members of the US Congress or the Indian Lok Sabha (the lower house of the Indian Parliament).

All of this is apart from the influence of the top political families ("princelings") who have long been in lucrative monopoly contracts with the state or paid with stakes in business projects facilitated by them; some juicy recent anecdotes on this are narrated in Desmond Shum's 2021 book *Red Roulette: An Insider's Story of Wealth, Power, Corruption and Vengeance in Today's China*. The ownership of many private companies is so murky and intertwined with public-sector companies that it is often difficult to keep track of the boundaries of the business-politics nexus. There have also been cases of successful private companies "persuaded" to invest billions of dollars in state-owned companies. There are also many crony capital deals between banks (particularly small- and medium-size ones) and private businesses.

The recent crackdowns on corruption may have reduced some egregious cases of malfeasance and conspicuous consumption, but members of what is called the red aristocracy, as long as they belong to the loyalist political factions, have been largely shielded. In any case, the overcentralization of power and increased nontransparency of political control have left the essential institutional channels of patronage and corruption intact, and may in some cases have substituted one set of crony capitalists for another. Meanwhile, making top bureaucrats nervous about arbitrary punishment from above has discouraged them from taking risky or bold decisions, leading to what is called lazy governance in China.

The business-politician nexus is, of course, quite common in India. As I have noted, about one-half of the current ruling party's members of Parliament (MPs) are businessmen; the corresponding percentage for MPs of all parties taken together is about one-fourth. The businessmen bring their own money for election campaigns and other political expenditure, and company donations to party funds for election are large, and—now, under the anonymous electoral bond system—openly nontransparent. In recent years crony oligarchs who are widely suspected of heavily contributing to the ruling party's coffers have received large regulatory favors.

Both countries have similar patterns of rampant influence peddling, policy manipulation, and politically connected firms getting favors—for example, in government contracts, loans from public banks, access to prize real estate, and monopoly mining rights. As China is more involved in massive construction and infrastructure activities, which are usually "rent-thick," there is more scope for corruption, as seems to be suggested by both anecdotal and empirical evidence. Raymond Fisman and Yongxiang Wang (2015) have detected corruption in state asset sales by comparing the prices of publicly traded assets to those of assets not traded publicly. There is some evidence, as noted by Yiming Cao (2021), that in the devastating 2008 Sichuan earthquake buildings constructed when the county officials had connections to their superiors at the prefecture level were 83 percent more likely to collapse relative to the no-connection benchmark. Such are the possible deadly consequences of the patronage system.

Let's take an example from a different area, public health: drug prices are usually much higher in China than in India, even though the single-payer system in Chinese health care should have given the government more bargaining power with the drug companies. People attribute this to the more entrenched kickback system between drug companies and doctors, hospitals, and officials in China.

It is likely that collusion between business and politics in governance is somewhat more subject to public scrutiny in India than in China, and the courts are somewhat more independent in India (though clogged and corrupt, particularly at the lower levels). The scrutiny of collusive behavior by Indian media is now, however, under a shadow with the concentration of its business ownership.

Additionally, as I have noted, relations with the all-powerful CCP can be somewhat precarious for Chinese business tycoons, as political disloyalty or even suspected independence is punished more harshly than in India. Indian politicians may be a bit more dependent on businessmen, particularly in view of election funding.

DECENTRALIZED STRUCTURES AND PRACTICES

A very distinctive feature of the Chinese governance system is that political centralization, in the imperial days as well as under the party in recent decades, has historically been tempered by a unique blending of political centralization with economic and administrative decentralization. Chenggang Xu (2011) has described the system as "regionally decentralized authoritarianism," in contrast with most authoritarian systems that are highly centralized.

India has been, in some sense, the obverse, combining political decentralization (regional power groupings have been quite strong, at least until the middle of the last decade) with economic centralization (with the regions dependent on central finance, the vertical fiscal imbalance is quite severe). In the last few years, though, centralization of power has reduced the influence of regional power groupings.

China has much better modes of managing infrastructure financing and construction at the local level. For example, urban infrastructure there is constructed, operated, and maintained by separate companies set up by the city government, whereas in India the municipal government tries to do this through its own departments. The latter are financially strapped, as they do not have much taxation power and are perpetually dependent on the state government for funds. In general, even after the centralizing reforms in 1994, the fiscal system is much more decentralized in China, where subprovincial levels of government tend to spend more than half of the total government budgetary expenditure, compared to only about 3 percent in India (not including the large off-budget revenue raising and expenditure of local governments in China). The much worse performance of subprovincial local bodies in India in the last-mile delivery of public services and facilities is partly attributable to this (even though local Chinese governments have also much larger responsibility for infrastructure building and public services). In India the emphasis has been more on fiscal transfers to local governments than on local tax autonomy.

In both China and India decentralization tends to accentuate regional inequality, though in India the constitutional body of the Finance Commission tends to partially compensate for this by allocating redistributive transfers to poorer regions.

In comparison with other developing countries, the Chinese local government is much more involved in local business development and not just in public services delivery. A few years back, when the private automaker Zhejiang Geely Holding Group bought up the Swedish car company Volvo in a widely publicized move, much of the money was actually provided by the local municipal government—something that would be unthinkable, for example, in India. Jurisdictional competition for mobile resources and business and regional competition in growth rates influencing career promotion of officials have usually played a much more important role in Chinese local development.

But in recent years the pace of experimentation and trial-and-error pilot projects in local areas, which characterized the early reform period, has slowed down. The current regime's more centralized, and personal-loyalty-based leadership has made experimentation even more difficult.

A growing literature in decentralization all over the world has pointed to the problem of the capture of local governments by the elite (including officials and intermediaries) and the frequent diversion of benefits and resources to nontarget groups.

In India there is plenty of evidence of landed interests undermining decentralized welfare programs for the poor, apart from state political administration and legislators hampering devolution of power to the municipalities and village councils. China's more egalitarian land use rights distribution after decollectivization may have prevented the rise of a landed oligarchy that has often captured local governments in parts of rural India.

Yet in recent decades Chinese decentralization has not been able to avoid the problem of serious local elite capture. Chinese local business, in collusion with local officials, has been at the root of problems of arbitrary land acquisition, toxic pollution, and violation of safety standards in food and in work for factories and mines. Such collusion is much more rampant in China than, say, in India, primarily because China has fewer checks from below on abuse of power.

On safety standards, for example, Chinese coal mine death rates are reported to be fifteen times higher than in India (and the death rate, even per unit of coal output, is much higher). On the basis of provincial-level panel data on key state coal mines in China from 1995 to 2005, Ruixhue Jia and Huihua Nie (2015) provide evidence that decentralization makes collusion between official regulators and firms more likely (in the Chinese media, such collusion is called *guan-mei goujie*) and is correlated with increases in coal mine fatality rates. This is also consistent with the general finding of Fisman and Wang (2015) that politically connected firms in China have higher rates of workplace fatalities based on firm-level data collected from different industries between 2008 and 2011. There is also suggestive evidence in Jia and Nie's study that media exposure can act as a deterrent against collusion. Monica Martinez-Bravo, and colleagues (2014) provide evidence, on the basis of village panel data, that local officials are better controlled by local elections than by central monitoring.

There are also fewer checks on debt-fueled overinvestment and excess capacity in local-government-controlled or politically connected firms (currently a source of major macroeconomic problems in China). China's central leadership is now trying to rein in the debt problem of local governments and their dependence on the shadow banking system.

My major purpose in this brief assessment of the strengths and weaknesses of the Chinese governance system has been to show that some of the positive features (like career incentives for officials to promote local development, or decentralized structure of management of infrastructure building and local business development) do not necessarily depend on the authoritarian system—they can very well be adopted, with proper reforms of organization and incentives, in a democratic country. Even the general ability of China's top leadership to quickly coordinate and mobilize the state machinery is not a feature of authoritarianism; note its absence in many authoritarian countries in Africa, Asia, or Latin America, and its vibrant presence in democratic Japan, South Korea, and Taiwan, not to speak of Scandinavia.

On the other hand, some of the major problems in Chinese governance arising from the lack of downward accountability—the choking of information flows delaying course correction in the case of serious decision-making mistakes; lack of open public scrutiny of corrupt collusion between officials and businessmen; and a systemic tendency in the face of a crisis to overreact, suppress information, and act heavy-handedly, thereby making the system less resilient—are all ugly features of authoritarianism that one should seriously take into account, even if one cares only about the performance of a system and not the intrinsic value of democratic freedom. One hopes that a consideration of these factors will help in resisting the allure of authoritarian capitalism that China is pushing as an alternative model.

5

The Slippery Slope of Majoritarianism

Even in countries that are not directly responding to the siren song of authoritarianism there is now a palpable tendency for democracies to be hollowed out by a crude form of majoritarianism—by white supremacists and Christian evangelicals in Brazil, Europe, Russia, and the United States; by Islamists in Indonesia, Pakistan, and Turkey; or by Hindu fanatics in India. They win votes, often in relatively free and fair elections, and declare the system democratic, even as they trash many of the liberal processes one usually associates with democracy. From Fareed Zakaria to Victor Orbán the new term that is being bandied about is the seemingly oxymoronic *illiberal democracy*. Is this different from elected authoritarianism?

A bit of definitional clarity on democracy is in order here. There are some political scientists (prominently, Adam Przeworski, following an idea originally proposed by Joseph Schumpeter in 1942) who use a "minimal" definition of democracy. They'd certify a polity as democratic if there are competitive elections in which the incumbent has a chance of being voted down. Others (including myself) would also insist on some basic minimum civil and political rights to be regularly enjoyed by citizens, and that there are some procedures of accountability in day-to-day administration under some overarching constitutional rules of the game. Those who are for the minimal definition would say that if citizens are dissatisfied with the performance of incumbents on the latter aspects, they can always throw them out in an election. But electoral sanctions are extremely blunt instruments, and there are many institutional practices that a democracy needs that may disappear in between elections.

Besides, elections themselves are fraught with problems; even ignoring that rampant gerrymandering and lopsided corporate donations to pro-business political parties make elections far less competitive, strong majoritarian leaders often prefer periodic renewals through acclamatory or referendum-style elections rather than multiple issue-based contests. They are also good at whipping up national security related frenzy just before election time. To give an example from India, in the most recent (2019) national election, in which Narendra Modi won a "landslide" victory, attention focused disproportionately on an incident of alleged terrorism and a tense confrontation with Pakistan, while many issues raised by social divisiveness and economic mismanagement in Modi's performance were drowned in a warlike mobilization. Citizens were expected to rally around the supreme leader, and to criticize him was openly branded as "antinational."

MINORITY RIGHTS: INDISPENSABLE FOR DEMOCRACY

In this chapter, I will focus on what I consider an indispensable non-electoral aspect of democracy: basic civic and political rights, particularly for minorities, which majoritarians often trample on in their onward march under the banner of electoral triumph. There is a special historical problem here in the origin of democracy that we want to highlight. Sharun Mukand and Dani Rodrik (2020), in an insightful article, detect a fundamental problem in the origin of the democratic political settlement. One popular account of this settlement in European history is that democracy came about as a compromise between the economic elite, interested in securing their property rights and afraid of mass upheavals, and the organized working classes and peasants who were clamoring for political rights. This led to the extension of the franchise and political representation, and to the rights to express, assemble, and organize, which ultimately led to welfare states of varying strengths.

The workers in their turn accepted some limits in their demands so that capitalist property rights and opportunities were essentially preserved. In this democratic settlement the economic elite had the strength of their wealth and the workers the strength of numbers. But the groups that lost out in this bargaining process (or never had a chance) were those who had neither wealth nor numbers—the various minority groups in society (defined by ethnicity, religion, ideology, language, gender identity, or sexual orientation). Way back in 1787 James Madison, in the *Federalist Papers,* rightly put the issue of minority rights at the center of democratic concern in a new republic. Today it has become the Achilles heel of liberal democracy where majorities are prone to tyrannize minorities. Of course, the legal hurdles that the United States puts up against tyranny of the majority are sometimes abused (when, for example, the electoral college system allows a president to get elected even while losing the popular vote in the national election by a large margin, or the US Senate practice of filibuster, through which a minority can repeatedly block legislation brought about by the majority party). But the principle of protection of minority, which is an important part of the US system, was a historic step in the right direction.

Mukand and Rodrik distinguish between political rights and civil rights, the latter largely relating to protection of minority groups (including protection of the rule of law, habeas corpus, and equal access to public services). They point out that in the aforementioned bargaining equilibrium between the economic elite and the majority of workers, those civil rights may simply be ignored and there may not be a strong enough group to fight for them or to make any credible threats to the other groups for their sustenance.

Some exceptions may take place when the ethnic minority is part of the economic elite (as in the case of Chinese businessmen in parts of Southeast Asia, or some Jewish Americans important in the business and media elite of their country), but even in these cases hate crimes and discrimination against such minority groups have not been uncommon. The situation is particularly acute when a major minority group is also among the poorest in the country (as a result of, for example, discrimination, social deprivation, or other causes), like the Muslims in India, or historically, Black people in the United States. A hundred years after the Civil War and Emancipation, Black Americans still remained largely disenfranchised, until a major civil rights movement in the 1960s, a concerted effort of many civil society organizations and active federal government support, brought about significant improvements in their basic rights. But the recent Black Lives Matter movement shows how much more there is still left to be done.

The distinction between political and civil rights is related to the distinction between *participatory* and *procedural* aspects of democracy that is often overlooked. As noted before, particularly in Chapters 1 and 3, majoritarian populists on either the right or the left usually ride roughshod over the procedural aspects (like the "due process" that minorities are entitled to under rule of law) or declare the opposition or the critical media as traitorous or an "enemy of the people." The question is, How does one preserve and sustain these procedural aspects?

SOCIAL DIVERSITY AND INSTITUTIONAL CHECKS AS SAFEGUARDS

An alternate way of looking at the origin of democracy—still keeping to an essentially interest-based (rather than idea-based) explanation—may provide a bit more hope for the political logic behind the sustenance of civil rights and the procedural aspects of liberal democracy. This alternative ascribes the rise of democracy to competition among different sections within the elite rather than the threat of mass uprisings faced by the elite as a whole. In my 1984 book *The Political Economy of Development in India,* I ascribed the survival of democracy in India, against a formidable set of odds, not so much to the strength of liberal values among the Indian population as to how—in a country of immense diversity—even the elite is so fragmented (with no element individually sufficiently strong to hijack the system by itself) that they agree on some minimum democratic rules in their transactional negotiations to keep their rivals at the bargaining table under some limits of moderation. Of course, when diversity or the lack of trust is extreme, the relevant formal and tacit agreements may unravel, and the rival groups may turn to civil war, as has often happened in Africa among clashing ethnic groups.

In that book I had referred to the nineteenth-century British example of the industrial bourgeoisie allowing an extension of franchise to the working classes, not necessarily out of love for or fear of them but more to checkmate their elite rivals in the landed aristocracy. Roughly similar, episodic, cases have been cited by political scientists in the history of Denmark, France, Greece, and Spain in the nineteenth century, and of Argentina and Portugal in the early part of the twentieth. In *Federalist Paper* no. 10, James Madison looked upon a great number of what he called "factions" (he was thinking of economic or social interest groups) and their diversity as the safeguard against tyranny. He pointed to "the greater security afforded by a greater variety of parties [i.e., 'factions'] against the event of any one party being able to outnumber and oppress the rest."

One, of course, needs an institutional structure to sustain civil rights, not just an informal standoff among factions. If elite fragmentation is such that each fragment is suspicious that some other fragment may get too powerful to endanger its civil rights, each party may then have a stake in a social contract that ensures some minimum framework of civil rights for everybody. This is somewhat akin to the Rawlsian theory of justice under a kind of "veil of ignorance," applied here to procedural rights. Mukand and Rodrik mention a somewhat similar case, a special situation in which there is no permanent majority or minority in society and coalitions keep shifting.

To make such a social contract binding, the elite fragments may then be interested in constitutions or other such founding documents that limit overreach on the part of anybody through arrangements like the separation of powers and checks and balances (subject to the limiting possibility that all the institutions are taken over by the same partisan interests). Institutions within the governmental setup (like the judiciary) and outside it (like the media, universities, and other civil society organizations) can become watchdogs against the abuse of power, particularly in the form of oppressing minorities.

In Brazil, Hungary, India, Israel, Turkey, the Philippines, Poland, Russia, and elsewhere, popularly elected governments are now systematically using their majoritarian muscles to weaken and intimidate the institutions that safeguard minority rights. In the United States these institutions, for all their faults, have been somewhat stronger all along, and in recent history offered a bit stiffer resistance against the then marauding president and his subservient party legislators, but even there the judiciary seems to be in the process of being captured by partisan political appointments and the media torn by sectarian polarization.

Yet, following the lines of Madison's thinking, it is the diversity of interest groups, regions, and identities and their collective action ability that may be the main source of lingering hope. Let me illustrate this in some detail with the case of an extremely diverse country like India. The Hindu nationalists currently enjoy many advantages in their onward march: a massive cadre-based and disciplined, though thoroughly bigoted, organization (the Rashtriya Swayamsevak Sangh, or RSS) attempting to forge cultural homogenization among the Hindus; a charismatic political leader not averse to using his bully pulpit to spread misleading half-truths, lies, and disinformation; access to a disproportionately large amount of corporate donations for election funds; and an infernal ability to use the arms of a preexisting, overextended state to harass and persecute dissidents and intimidate the rest (through, for instance, ample use of investigative and tax-raiding agencies, misuse of colonial-era sedition laws against critics of the government, threats of the withdrawal of public advertisements from critical media outlets, and allowing impunity for the partisan lynch mobs or police against minorities).

It is widely suspected that the RSS has also infiltrated parts of the police force and army, so they are complicit in Hindu nationalist antics (just as in the United States white supremacists seem to have successfully infiltrated parts of the military and law enforcement—to which the US Departments of Defense and Justice have recently woken up—particularly after some of them participated in the riots on the US Capitol on January 6, 2021). The atmosphere of fear and intimidation in India has immobilized many civil society groups. Labor unions, once a possible center of organized opposition, have been in a kind of structural decline. Sadly, even the judiciary seems to have been compromised, and it is often timid or erratic. And the government has been helped by the feckless and disorganized nature of the opposition political parties.

Nevertheless, in the long term the odds are against such drastic homogenization and the cramming of the manifold diversities of Hindu society into the Procrustean bed of an invented, artificial, poisonous, and religious nationalism—against which Mahatma Gandhi, the father of the nation, fought throughout much of his life. Hinduism has never been an organized or standardized religion, and in a country of extreme linguistic, cultural, and other diversities and powerful centrifugal forces, the project of suppressing the civil rights of the world's largest minority population in any one country (nearly two hundred million

Muslims, apart from other dissidents) is unlikely to be viable over a long period—at least not without giving up all semblance of democracy.

Social movements for group and regional autonomy and political movements for more decentralization and devolution of power are likely to grow in reaction. Already the arbitrary division of the state of Kashmir and military lockdown and assault on the dignity of the people there have almost completely alienated them. The anti-Muslim Citizenship Amendment Act and the proposed National Registry of Citizens for the whole country have provoked widespread unrest, often led by women. In early 2020—before the COVID-19 pandemic dispersed them—it was invigorating to see, in the streets of different parts of India, diverse crowds of young people gathered by the thousands, chanting the preamble to the liberal-pluralistic Constitution of India, even though a repressive government continued to use violence and intimidation against protesters. In the near future, civil disobedience movements and regional resistance against arbitrary laws that seem to violate the spirit, if not always the letter, of the constitution are likely to grow and provide formidable opposition.

In 2021 a substantial movement of North Indian farmers against the government's farm laws attracted international attention and, after a year of sustained protests, won a repeal of those laws. Even though many of them had mixed feelings about some of the movement's demands, a majority of their supporters agreed that the laws were arbitrarily formulated and rammed through the Indian Parliament without consultation with the stakeholders and that the government treatment of the protesters have been heavy-handed and callous.

In general, to be effective the brewing opposition needs to be organized on all fronts: in the legislatures, in the media, and in the streets, and by the state governments that are still controlled by opposition parties. For far too long even the opposition states have allowed the central government to usurp powers arbitrarily to assault the basic structure of the constitution in many ways; reorganize and overhaul some states; violate the spirit of federalism in not involving or consulting the state governments while ramming through crucial legislations on policing, law and order and social welfare services (all of which constitutionally are state subjects); change the terms of reference of the constitutional body of the Finance Commission, which allocates resources between the central and state governments; introduce questionable forms of election funding; and so on. Even when the central government's actions are technically legal, one could follow Gandhi, who taught Indians to organize mass civil disobedience when the laws are not socially legitimate.

Such movements may command attention when started with refreshing bursts of spontaneity and vigor and authenticity of decentralized leaderlessness, but to gather steam and ultimately sustain momentum over the medium to long term they'll need some coordination and direction, particularly from some degree of association with mass organizations (the farmers' protest had some North Indian farmer organizations working for them), a minimum common agenda for diverse groups, and youthful leaders.

This is an example of an uphill battle for protecting the essence of liberal democracy that liberals all over the world should keep a vigilant eye on. It is vitally important, particularly at a time when the Achilles heel of liberal democracy everywhere looks grievously exposed.

6

Social Democracy Redux

In this chapter and Chapter 7 we will explore the feasibility and desirability of drawing upon the old idea of social democracy to address the current crisis of liberal democracy and of modifying it in the context of new technology and the institutional demands of evolving capitalism. In order to differentiate our proposed social democracy from some of the actual, often discredited, political practice in its name, in this chapter we will first explore the general idea of social democracy as holding a kind of ideological balance between different social values and between the alternative social coordination mechanisms through which society strives toward those values. We will then go into the reasons for the decline of the so-called social democratic parties in recent decades, and into ways of reviving social democracy under the constraints and opportunities of a new postpandemic world. In Chapter 7 we'll examine the fraught relationship between social democracy and capitalism, and how to restructure both to the benefit of all stakeholders—capital, labor, and the community of involved citizens.

Given the breakdown of the old class compromise that formed the basis of social democracy, one needs to work on a delicate reconfiguration.

As the precarity of work, and of life in general, have increased in recent years, social democracy—with its main promise of providing economic security and social solidarity—may have some chance of renewal now. With increased awareness (particularly among young people) of the positive role of the state, and new technology increasing the capacity of the state to reach out to people even at the margins of society and to strengthen the organizational capacity of activists who protest the iron grip of big-money lobbies, that chance of renewal is not so remote.

SOCIAL DEMOCRACY AS AN IDEOLOGICAL BALANCING ACT

Let us move beyond the overly simple and amorphous Left versus Right distinction of common ideological parlance, which historically originated in particular ways of seating in the French National Assembly. Over the years the distinction has become quite misleading, particularly in failing to capture the multidimensionality of ideological positions. Let us instead start with the old-style foundational values of liberty, equality, and fraternity. The old, simple categorization used to be that those who emphasize the primacy of liberty as a social value were called liberals; a belief in the primacy of equality or social justice used to be associated with socialists; and belief in the primacy of fraternity or community solidarity led one to be described as a communitarian. But there are multiple layers in that trinity of social values, and people usually mix the ingredients of all three in their belief systems in markedly varying proportions to concoct a smorgasbord that passes for their ideology.

I should also point out that we are discussing here only somewhat idealized versions of ideological positions, not actual behavior. There are routinely, of course, large gulfs between people's professed beliefs and the reality of their conduct. We'll refrain here, for example, from the easier task of legitimately castigating many liberals of the last two hundred years for being complicit in racist or imperialist depredations, just as we are not going to spend time here in reproaching many social democrats for various machinations and corrupt or self-serving deals that were contrary to the genuine interests of the working class that they professed to uphold.

Liberty

There is a tradition among philosophers to distinguish between negative and positive forms of liberty—the former denoting *freedom from* undue intervention or restrictions, and the latter denoting *freedom to* do things that enhance one's self-realization and well-being. Libertarians are preoccupied with the former, democratic socialists often with the latter. Social democrats want a bit of both. To confound matters, there are those who describe themselves as "left libertarians" and combine attachment to individual freedom with an egalitarian approach to natural resources. Some of them are opposed to the private ownership of means of production, and others are skeptical of the private ownership of natural resources, arguing in contrast to right-wing libertarians that neither claiming nor mixing one's labor with natural resources is enough to generate the claim to full private property rights.

People also distinguish between economic freedom and political freedom. The former primarily relates to private property rights and the relatively unhindered operation of private initiative and enterprise, and the latter to rights to free expression and democratic participation.

Milton Friedman openly gave economic freedom primacy over political freedom. In his 1994 introduction to the fiftieth anniversary edition of F. A. Hayek's *Road to Serfdom,* he categorically stated, "The free market is the only mechanism that has ever been discovered for achieving participatory democracy." In this Friedman seems to have gone beyond the line of thought expressed in his classic 1962 book *Capitalism and Freedom,* where he stated, "History suggests only that capitalism is a necessary condition for political freedom. Clearly it is not a sufficient condition." His 1994 statement implies that economic freedom is a necessary *and* sufficient condition for political freedom. I think that Friedman was generally wrong in this. There are some countries (or long periods in the history of a country) that were politically democratic without much in the way of free markets (the first four decades of independent India can be cited as an example), and there are many undemocratic countries with a lot of free market enterprise. In the Heritage Foundation's Economic Freedom Index for 2022, the top position is occupied by Singapore, with United Arab Emirates among those described as "mostly free" countries, and Bahrain, Hungary, Poland and Vietnam ranked as "moderately free." None of these six countries has distinguished itself in terms of political freedom. This suggests that economic freedom is neither a necessary nor a sufficient condition for political freedom.

I should recount here an interaction I had with Friedman himself on a related issue many years back. At a conference in which both of us were invited speakers Friedman attributed the then widely acclaimed postwar advance of the Japanese economy, in contrast to the relative stagnation of the Indian economy, to the regulations and controls in the latter and to their absence in the former. I pointed out to him that the Japanese state was not particularly a paragon of noninterference. His answer, unfalsifiable as it happened to be, was that the Japanese economy would have done even better without the state interference.

Economic freedom is often described as a key characteristic of the capitalist system. But, somewhat paradoxically for liberal believers in capitalism, the most successful recent case of what many would describe as capitalism is from China under the leadership of the so-called Chinese Communist Party, where there is considerable economic freedom, though political freedom is largely absent. While most of the

Chinese economy—and particularly its dynamic parts—is in the private sector, both in production and employment, the state provides overarching guidance and control. The success of capitalism is now closely associated with nationalist glory. The Chinese leadership can undo individual capitalists at short notice (in recent years some of the richest men in China have been put in jail or faced crackdowns), but the important systemic issue is that it will find it much more difficult to undo a whole network of capitalist relations, by now thickly overlaid with vested interests at various levels. As China (like Vietnam) is no longer a plausible example of socialism, it is now hard for anticapitalists to find a significant case of a durably viable and technologically dynamic economy that is run on traditional socialist lines of control. Yet, of course, many dream on.

Economic freedom is associated with market competition, and competition is meaningless if it is not on a level playing field. Thus, liberals who support economic freedom should be in favor of vigorous measures to curb monopoly and business collusion, though not all liberals do this with alacrity. Raghuram Rajan and Luigi Zingales, in their 2003 book *Saving Capitalism from the Capitalists,* show how in the United States entrenched incumbents, particularly in financial markets, use their power to protect their own economic position and to repress the same free market through which they originally achieved success. It is part of a dialectical relationship between capitalists and markets in which capitalists, after entering a market, try their best to raise barriers to entry for others. Friedman often used to dismiss the importance of empirical cases of monopoly except those brought about or protected by government action. This overlooks many important cases where technology, economies of scale, and network effects generate durable monopoly businesses without much involvement by the government (in today's world, Facebook and Google are obvious examples).

Liberals, in emphasizing the importance of individual rights and autonomy, recognize the equal dignity of every human being. But there are at least two ways these individual rights come into conflict with the rights of a collectivity of individuals in some democracies. First, in many divided societies identity groups are so politically powerful that their group rights can sometimes suppress individual freedoms in quite unwarranted ways. For example, in such societies a book, film, or artwork may be banned if there is even a whiff of a suspicion that it may offend the sensibilities of some ethnic or religious group, trampling in the process on an individual's democratic freedom of expression. A liberal sensitive to identity issues is often torn in this matter. Second, in many countries where there is an overwhelmingly large majority group along with relatively small identity- or culture-based minorities, there is a danger of democracy degenerating into a kind of crude majoritarianism—a phenomenon that, as I noted in Chapter 5, is now quite common under the leadership of populist demagogues in Brazil, Hungary, India, the Philippines, Poland, Russia, Turkey, and elsewhere. A liberal in this context is often pitted against elected authoritarianism.

Finally, as I noted in Chapter 2, for many people liberalism, in privileging individual autonomy and freedom, often leaves a social and emotional vacuum that conservatives are more adept at filling. Conservatives can evoke a sense of belonging to a larger community, even a sense of solidarity that liberals obsessed with individual rights—or, more recently, with the individual dignity and "recognition" aspects of identity politics—cannot inspire. We'll come back to this issue of fraternity and community later in this chapter.

Equality

The conflict between liberty and equality is often central to ideological differences among social scientists. This conflict was pointed out most eloquently by B. R. Ambedkar, a major architect of the Indian Constitution and a leader of a historically disadvantaged community in India, in his last speech in the Constituent Assembly before the Indian Constitution was set to start operating on January 26, 1950:

> On the 26th of January 1950, we are going to enter into a life of contradictions. . . . In politics we will be recognizing the principle of one man one vote and one vote one value. In our social and economic life, we shall, by reason of our social and economic structure, continue to deny the principle of one man one value. How long shall we continue to live this life of contradictions? How long shall we continue to deny equality in our social and economic life? If we continue to deny it for long, we will do so only by putting our political democracy in peril.

This contradiction is now acute in many democracies as economic inequality has reached grotesquely high levels.

What may have been uppermost in Ambedkar's mind was the social inequalities of India, where low castes had been subject to centuries of oppression, humiliation, and discrimination. Such inequalities are clearly inconsistent with the equal dignity of human beings that the concepts of liberty and democracy connote. The past seventy years in India have shown that political equality of democracy can bring about substantial, even dramatic, changes in access to political power for some hitherto subordinate groups, though vast numbers of the underprivileged continue to remain victims of social and economic inequality. (The last thirty years of the South African case show similar results.)

Economic inequality, whether in income or wealth, can also have a direct adverse impact on the quality and quantity of democracy. For example, there is a popular argument in comparative history, emphasized by the political sociologist Barrington Moore in his 1966 landmark study, that traditional forms of land inequality, which concentrate power in a landed elite, make the emergence of democracy difficult.

Similarly, looking at the contrasting development paths in North and South America since early colonial times, the economic historians Kenneth Sokoloff and Stanley Engerman (2000) have shown how societies with high land inequality at the outset of colonialization (particularly with factor endowments suited to plantation agriculture, with slave labor or minerals that could be extracted with forced labor) develop institutions that restrict access to political power to a narrow elite and block the transition to democracy.

Even where wealth comes from sources other than land, economic inequality enables the rich and the corporate sector to pour resources into the political influence machine to get the system to work in their favor, particularly through lobbying, media shaping, and campaign financing. All of this often results in laws and regulations, along with tax cuts, that favor even further wealth concentration and the perpetuation of plutocratic power, either undermining democracy or allowing a kind of sham democracy in which economic inequality cripples genuine political freedom and competition.

Some egalitarians even go to the extreme of suggesting that in countries with high inequality and poverty, liberty is essentially vacuous, mainly allowing the dispossessed multitudes the "freedom to starve," for they contrast the *bourgeois democracy* of capitalist countries and the *people's democracy* of more egalitarian countries. With the generally sad experience of many decades of people's democracies in communist countries in the recent past, it is probably correct instead to take the conceptual position that liberty retains some intrinsic value even independent of the value of equality. Similarly, advocates of social justice find in egalitarian policies the attempt to fulfill some ethical norms that may be independent of other values like liberty.

Liberals, of course, point out that government policies to redress inequality can hurt liberty—for example, when the disincentive effects of progressive taxation to pay for redistributive policies limit the economic freedom for private enterprise, investment, and risk taking.

There is clearly an important trade-off here, even if one ignores some cases of socially unproductive risk taking by the rich (with "collateral damage" for the poor)—for example, in financial or real estate speculation. The general social consensus in different countries takes different forms on this trade-off.

Many conservatives advocate an environment of low taxes, light regulation, and low government spending as conducive to private initiative and innovations. Social democrats, however, point out that the relatively high tax to gross domestic product (GDP) ratio in social democratic countries, which funds a generous welfare state and a more sturdy physical and social infrastructure, has not hurt the cause of liberty. The Cato Institute's Human Freedom Index (2021) as a measure of personal freedom is actually higher in the Nordic countries (and in some other welfare states like the Netherlands and New Zealand) than in the United States. It has also actually helped the cause of business innovations, and it seems that a well-provided-for, healthy, educated, and more stable and satisfied labor force has improved productivity and profitability. (For more on this, see Chapter 7.)

It has also been pointed out that even in the United States much basic or foundational research and many great innovations of recent times (like the internet, GPS, digital search engines, supercomputers, the Human Genome Project, magnetic resonance imaging, and smartphone technology), which private business has turned to profitable use, have been facilitated by or been the outcome of public investment funded to a large extent by taxpayers. In the context of the recent COVID-19 pandemic it has been reported (for example in the *Washington Post,* May 26, 2020, and on National Public Radio, June 29, 2020) that in the development of Remdesivir, an antiviral treatment, taxpayers provided more than $70 million over the past two decades, and yet the private biotech company Gilead Sciences, after acquiring the drug, was charging at the rate of $3,120 for a five-day course of it.

It has been widely observed that people's attitudes to inequality differ according to their belief in the relative importance of *luck* versus *effort* in an individual's doing financially well, a belief that varies from one social context to another. Conservatives emphasize the importance of effort. In a related context, liberals also raise the issue of personal responsibility in discussing the kinds of inequality that are morally permissible. The latter, for example, may pertain to cases where, when two individuals face similar life chances, one ends up richer than the other simply because the former is more ambitious or hardworking than the latter. This brings to the fore a distinction between inequality of opportunity and of outcome.

As philosophers, social commentators, and the general public increasingly find the issue of personal responsibility in one's choice or life decisions quite socially salient, one should make a clear distinction between *opportunity egalitarianism* and *outcome egalitarianism*. The former seeks to offset only those inequalities that are due to circumstances beyond an individual's control (like the characteristics of a family or neighborhood a child is born in or its biological characteristics). The latter seeks to offset even those differences in outcome that are due to an individual's own choice (e.g., in blowing away one's opportunity by indulging in drugs or alcohol) or initiative (or lack thereof). The distinction, of course, gets a bit more complicated when one keeps in mind issues of intergenerational inequality, as you have to ensure equality of opportunity between children of ambitious or enterprising parents and children of "slacker" parents.

It is worth noting that some liberals' support of meritocracy is undercut when one looks at it from the point of view of opportunity egalitarianism. What these liberals ascribe to merit turns out to be often the result of a combination of a set of unequal opportunities in the form of better home environments, neighborhoods, and social networks, landing them with better (at least from the credentialing point of view) educational institutions and job contacts. Such structural advantages masquerading as earned merit are, of course, much more acute in countries with a long history of race or caste oppression.

Fraternity and Community

Some social thinkers ascribe a great deal of value to fraternity or the bonds with the community in which one is embedded. This community may include the family, kin groups, neighborhood, all the way up to the political community of the nation—all collectivities with which some issues of the individual's identity may be involved. I have already mentioned that conservatives drawing upon community traditions have tried to deflate the universalistic pretentions of liberalism. As was noted in Chapter 2, communitarian philosophers like Charles Taylor have criticized what they call the "atomism" of the libertarian concept of self and suggested that the moral commitments that define our identity and meaning may arise from the social world in which we are located.

In real life, fraternity and community can, however, be in serious conflict with both liberty and equality. As was noted in Chapter 2, traditional patriarchal families or kinship groups can be quite authoritarian in their treatment—particularly of younger and female members. The latter, for example, have to accept many restrictions on their choice of work associates and marriage partners, sanctions on departures from due deference to the aged leaders, and injunctions on sharing the benefits from individual efforts and innovations. Furthermore, compared to larger social entities where many rival groups contend, small local community institutions may be more susceptible to capture by local overlords, oligarchs, and majoritarian tyrants—as with white supremacists in the localities of the US South, the tyranny of dominant castes in Indian villages, or Mafia capture of local institutions in Sicily. In all of these cases, outside intervention has been necessary to relieve institutionalized systems of local oppression.

Today, all over the world, community-grown identity fanatics following populist demagogues are trying to thwart liberals who display more openness to ethnic minorities and immigrants. Even some (though not all) social democrats in rich countries feel that they have to be responsive to the cultural anxiety on the issues of immigration and multiculturalism expressed by the working classes. Not all "social justice warriors" worry about global justice, as there can be conflicts in the interests of the working classes of rich and poor countries.

Social Coordination Mechanisms

Ideological positions vary not just with respect to the different weights people put on aspects of liberty, equality, and fraternity but also in important ways relating to the three major social coordination mechanisms society uses in functioning and striving toward those values: the *state,* the *market,* and the local *community.* The merits of the state versus the market is, of course, a staple of old Left versus Right debates. Even on the so-called Left, social democrats sharply differ from socialists on the role of the market and private capital. Among social democrats who allow the mode of production to be mainly capitalist, there are significant differences between those who want the state to be the main funder, but not necessarily the actual provider, of essential public services like education, health, water supply, and public transportation (in recent decades even Nordic social democracies have expanded the range of choices in providers of public services), and those who think that some essential quality in those public services is lost if they are left to profit-making private agencies to provide. On the other hand, particularly in developing countries, state officials may be inept, truant, or corrupt, and the political accountability mechanisms are often much too weak to discipline them; under the circumstances, some public-private competition may be bracing.

As noted at the end of Chapter 2, in their advocacy of a strong state the state socialists are sometimes in the uncomfortable company of jingoistic right-wing nationalists. In limiting the job-displacing effects of globalization, pursuing autarchic trade restrictions, and promoting state-directed industrial policy, the Right and the Left sometimes merge in the policy arena. The increasing precariousness of work and the rise of all kinds of insecurity as a result of the COVID-19 pandemic have made state effectiveness in social protection seem more imperative to people on all sides, though there are some differences among liberals and social democrats on the issue of protecting particular jobs versus protecting incomes.

On the operation of the market mechanism there are differences among liberals. There are those who follow the traditional economics textbook idea of small agents relentlessly competing, guided by an invisible hand toward an efficient allocation of resources (barring some spillover effects from individual actions). Other liberals and social democrats think that the market, though valuable in itself, is operated by large, clunky bureaucratic entities called corporate firms with necessarily incomplete contracts (where performance or quality cannot be prespecified in enforceable contracts) and subject to highly imperfect financial discipline, resulting in neither efficiency nor equity. Social democrats also emphasize that the labor market is qualitatively different from other markets, such as the market for vegetables—it acts more like a social institution where values of fairness, reciprocity, responsibility, and dignity matter. In such a world, markets and sociopolitical processes are intertwined and demands for democratizing firm's governance become salient. (There will be more on this in Chapter 7.)

In poor countries, liberals are also divided on the issue of how best to alleviate poverty. Some liberals mainly depend on market-fueled economic growth to raise incomes and jobs for the poor (so called trickle-down economics), whereas social democrats find this inadequate and stress the role of the state in pushing through substantial antipoverty programs. Even right-wing people now by and large accept (more so, say, in Europe and India than in the United States) the need for adequate welfare policies for the poor, though they may worry about the inefficiency, waste, and perverse work incentives in some of the programs. On trade policy, liberals and most social democrats are generally in favor of trade liberalization, particularly on the grounds of keeping imported inputs cheaper and for external competition acting as a disciplining force on domestic product costs and quality, whereas socialists and the radical Right may insist on more autarchic policies enabling "learning by doing" and self-reliance.

Among the Right, there are sharp differences between greed-is-good market fundamentalists, on the one hand, and conservatives, on the other, who dread the encroachments of the market on traditional family values and community dislocations, as much as those encroachments following from distant bureaucratic interventions. Contrary to popular impression, neither Margaret Thatcher nor her guru F. A. Hayek were conservative in this sense—Hayek even wrote a well-known essay titled "Why I am Not a Conservative."

Among communitarians, at one end there are those who are anti-state anarchists and libertarians (in the United States, sometimes fighting for their gun rights) and those who are against all hierarchy; at the other end there are those who are comfortable with stable, placid communities held up by hierarchy and deference. Those who are not against the state, but only against centralized state power, sometimes want more devolution of authority to local governments that can be more responsive to local needs and aspirations. At the same time, decentralized local governments are sometimes captured (they may be easier to capture than central governments), and when the weak are thereby oppressed by the local powerful, appeals to central authorities for protection and relief are not uncommon. As I noted in Chapter 2, in his book *Two Cheers for Anarchism*, the political scientist James C. Scott endorses many of the anarchist ideas on the independent self-organizing power of individuals and small communities for informal coordination without hierarchy, but he recognizes that the state is not always the enemy of freedom and that the relative equality that is necessary for small group coordination and mutuality can often only be guaranteed through the state.

All of this illustrates how the complexities around the three coordination mechanisms of the state, the market, and the community can give rise to a whole panoply of ideological positions. Those mechanisms can all do superb coordination jobs in specific contexts and fail utterly in others: we are all familiar with cases of government failures, market failures and community failures. The mechanisms all have their strengths and weaknesses, and the different ideological positions that thinking people often take reflect different prior empirical judgments about their relative importance in different historical contexts. To many thinkers and political leaders who are in search of some pragmatic balance among the social values of liberty, equality, and fraternity, and among the three social coordination mechanisms of state, market, and community, social democracy often seems like the embodiment of an imperfect but acceptable compromise. So there is a chance that in the tussle of ideas and interests in our complex world it will survive despite its current decline in different parts of the world, to which we now turn.

THE RECENT DECLINE OF SOCIAL DEMOCRATIC POLITICS

Long before the COVID-19 pandemic, social democratic parties in different parts of the world—including Brazil, Europe, India, Turkey, and the United States—had been on a long losing streak, yielding power or at least a large part of the political space to mostly right-wing populist parties. (There are now some signs of possible revival of social democrats in Germany and the Iberian Peninsula.) There have been a few cases of left-wing populism in Latin America; even in social democracies there, like Chile, public distrust and protests, and the recent election of a left-wing president, have been associated with inequality and decline of public services. In the United States, where the safety net for workers has been patchy compared to that in western Europe, it became much weaker, with cuts in government expenditure in recent decades, even as the need for it mounted. Data from the US Bureau of Labor Statistics (2020) suggest that between 1999 and 2019 the number of Americans aged twenty-five to fifty-four who are outside the labor force grew by 25 percent, or 4.7 million—over six times more than the number who received help from the main assistance program for displaced workers.

This has also been a period of decline for traditional working-class trade unions; for example, since 1985 trade union membership has halved on average across the member countries of the Organisation for Economic Co-operation and Development (OECD). With automation and globalization many traditional jobs have disappeared, and workers have lost much of their faith in the power of trade unions to safeguard their interests. Yet they are increasingly suffering in low-paying, back-breaking jobs with relentless productivity quotas and surveillance routines. Various business interests run persistent and well-funded campaigns against unions and have captured the attention of much of the media and many think tanks, succeeding in shrinking organized workers' traditional rights and domain—from the right-to-work movement pushed by employers (which undermines the unions' ability to fund themselves) in the US Rust Belt to the hiring of large numbers of contract laborers without benefits to work side by side with regular workers in factories in India. (In Europe, where the bargaining is often not at the individual firm level but at the industry or sectoral level, there is less incentive on the part of business to try to weaken unions at the firm level, but then there is a "free rider" problem among individual workers, as they can get the bargained benefits without paying the dues for union membership.)

Technological and demographic change have also been at work in shifting the support base of social democratic parties. Let me mention two kinds of change here. The first is the way technological change and the spread of education and the knowledge economy made a significant fraction of the workforce more professional, skilled, or at least white-collar. In their work patterns, income profile, lifestyles, assortative mate selections, and residence in gentrified parts of cities, these white-collar workers are increasingly different from the older, less educated, often socially more conservative blue-collar workers who used to be the mainstay of traditional unions. In Western countries white-collar workers have provided much of the support base for the type of politics associated with Tony Blair, Bill Clinton, Barack Obama, and Emmanuel Macron, which has driven away significant numbers of the blue-collar workers disillusioned about social democratic parties. White-collar politics has often connived at some pruning of the welfare state and public services, macroeconomic austerity policies, trade and financial liberalization, and openness to immigration and to diversity of identity groups (based on race, gender, or sexual orientation)—all of which have in one way or another alienated many blue-collar workers.

Thomas Piketty, in his book *Capital and Ideology,* cites data to show that between 1950 and 1970 support for the Democratic Party in the United States and various left-wing parties in Europe was stronger among people with the lowest education levels, but in the twenty years since 2000, support for such parties has become associated more with people with the highest level of education. While Piketty has mocked what he calls the "Brahminical" attitude of the centrist liberals, it is likely that the structural reason of the technological-demographic divide may be more at the root of the fragmentation of working-class support of social democratic parties. As I have indicated in preceding chapters, blue-collar workers, resentful of their cultural and economic distance from the more liberal social democratic workers, have turned to populist leaders and demagogues who give voice to their resentment, xenophobia, distrust of experts, and majoritarian inclinations to trample upon procedural niceties of liberal democracy like due process or minority rights. In India, Indonesia, and Turkey such majoritarianism has taken the form of Hindu or Islamic fanaticism and intolerance against their respective Muslim, Chinese, or Kurd minorities. The large corruption scandals in the social democratic party regimes in Brazil and India (of the Partido dos Trabalhadores and the Congress Party, respectively) also helped in sealing their fate.

The second change in the composition of the working class has involved the rising numerical importance of service, retail, and caregiving workers (added to them now are many of the "gig economy" workers) compared to workers in the declining or stagnating manufacturing and transportation sectors. On account of the locational dispersion of workplaces, the former are more difficult to organize and are left out of traditional unions; as a result they now form an underclass of underpaid workers (in spite of the good organizational work done by service worker unions like the Service Employees International Union [SEIU] in the United States and Canada, or UNI Europa in Europe). This has reinforced the fragmentation of the labor movement that social democrats used to give leadership to.

In developing countries the additional reason for labor fragmentation is the large divide between the formal and informal parts of the economy. A substantial proportion of workers, sometimes the majority (and an overwhelming majority in India, Kenya, and Peru), are informal, without any organization or benefits. Many of these informal workers are self-employed and are often less interested in wage-bargaining issues (which form the staple of union activities) than in getting credit, insurance, marketing, supply networks, infrastructural facilities, and protection from extortionate police or inspectors to support their production activities. Social democratic parties have not succeeded in creating unifying platforms that can build a bridge between formal and informal workers.

CONSTRAINTS AND OPPORTUNITIES IN A
POSTPANDEMIC WORLD

The COVID-19 pandemic has left large scars on the economy and society. In the poorer parts of the world it is estimated that millions of people may have reentered the zone of extreme poverty as a result of the economic crisis that followed the pandemic. It is possible that the pandemic, combined with US-China-Russia geopolitical tension, has weakened some of the forces of globalization, with people becoming more concerned about dependence on outside sources for some essential products like food, medicine, medical equipment, and semiconductor chips, or in general on supply chains vulnerable to disruption. (The war in Ukraine and international sanctions on Russia have particularly hurt developing countries dependent on imports of oil, fertilizers and wheat.) But in the long run, these concerns are likely to lead to greater diversification of trade outlets, not necessarily less international trade, and one should not underestimate the resilience of global value chains. Some American or European jobs in labor-intensive industries lost to China may now go to Vietnam and other Southeast Asian countries. Additionally, while the general climate of economic insecurity is likely to reinforce the demand for more domestic production and jobs and reduce enthusiasm for specialization by comparative advantage, it should be clear that in today's economy of integrated global value chains and the continuous swapping of parts, components, and tasks across borders, a large-scale retreat from relatively free trade will be harmful even for domestic jobs in most countries. Of course, as the pandemic has reminded us, open trade policies have to be combined with adequate social insurance for those who may lose out. In countries without the latter the political and economic effects of trade can be highly disruptive.

A retreat from multilateral international institutions, like a retreat from trade, would also be costly for most countries—particularly the poorer countries, which would be at the mercy of powerful countries in bilateral negotiations. This is not to say, however, that those institutions and the policies they promote do not need reform. The rules by which multilateral institutions operate were disproportionately shaped by corporate lobbies from rich countries, and do not do enough to help workers (or social democrats). And the usual stampede of capital from developing countries at the first sign of a crisis should make those countries even more wary of policies that favor capital-account liberalization. In any case, social democrats in rich and poor countries alike, even those who generally support unrestricted trade, should not be supportive of free international mobility of capital, which in the absence of such mobility for labor reduces labor's relative bargaining power.

The mobility of labor is itself a sensitive matter. In rich countries, social democrats have to be flexible about immigration and prepared to compromise on parts of the demands of the domestic working class. It is easy for liberals in the professional classes to be generous about supporting unrestricted immigration, but they cannot completely ignore the concerns of poorer workers, which often include minorities and recent immigrants (in the United States many African Americans and even Hispanics are more supportive of some restrictions on immigration than are richer liberals). With some patience and finesse one can work out delicate compromises on this issue without shutting the door to immigration. (In Chapters 3 and 9, I briefly discuss examples of such compromises.)

But as much as globalization and its discontents may hurt labor, workers may get hit even harder by labor-replacing automation and digital technology, both of which have been boosted by the pandemic, which has discouraged the congregation of large numbers of workers. A February 2021 McKinsey Global Institute study of eight countries (covering some OECD countries, as well as China and India) on the impact of the pandemic on future work patterns suggests that the largest negative impact is to fall on workers in food service and customer sales and service roles, as well as less-skilled office support roles. Jobs in warehousing and transportation may increase as a result of the growth in e-commerce and the delivery economy, but those increases are unlikely to offset the disruption of many other low-wage jobs. Thus, with the net effect of these forces likely to be negative for low-skill, low-wage jobs, and with continuing pressure from widespread unemployment and underemployment, union leaders and other labor activists will continue to struggle to organize and mobilize workers in large numbers. Another structural factor that will reduce the bargaining power of labor is the pandemic's likely effect on corporate concentration as large firms with deep pockets gain over the small.

While remote-working professionals and the digital-technology-based knowledge economy will grow in importance, continuing the changing nature of support for the social democratic parties, there may be some revitalizing forces generated by renewed efforts to organize the retail and service workers, as there is increased recognition of the importance of so-called essential workers and how underpaid and underprotected they are. In developing countries, where the majority of workers are informal, the increased awareness in the face of economic crisis of their lack of minimum economic security may encourage efforts by labor organizations to find a bridge between formal and informal workers in terms of common demands—like universal health care and some form of universal basic income, which may then form an important agenda and support structure for social democratic parties.

As I pointed out in Chapter 1, unlike in the United States, the right-wing populist parties elsewhere (like Alternative für Deutschland in Germany, Prawo i Sprawiedliwość in Poland, or even Rassemblement National in France) are also avid supporters of the welfare state. The right-wing ruling party in India, the Bharatiya Janata Party, while initially mocking the Congress Party about its welfare ("dole") schemes of public food distribution and rural employment guarantee on public works, has not merely continued with these schemes but has added programs for the provision of subsidized cooking fuel, financially inclusive measures like bank accounts for the poor, urban housing, and a (very modest) minimum income supplement for farmers. In order to differentiate its products from those on the right, social democrats have to be innovative not just in "redistribution" but also in the sphere of production or what is sometimes called predistribution. This might mean modifying corporate structures by, for example, giving workers more voice in the firm's governance, by giving labor a role in choosing the pattern of new technology to be adopted, in negotiations on international trade agreements, or in legislation to curb domestic monopolies (more on these in Chapter 7).

SOCIAL DEMOCRACY IN A WORLD OF HEIGHTENED INEQUALITY AND INSECURITY

Of course, the need for redistribution will be pressing as the pandemic exacerbates the forces of inequality in manifold ways—more greatly afflicting the poor, in their dense, squalid, and vulnerable living conditions, and with asymmetry in the vaccine rollout. The lockdowns destroyed their jobs quickly, with little social protection (which was patchy and job connected in the United States and almost nonexistent in poor countries) and with underfunded and underequipped public health systems. Many small businesses of the self-employed collapsed, with lost skills and low educational background of workers making their labor market adaptability difficult. There is the gaping digital divide between workers who can work remotely and the majority who cannot. For the long term, these forces may be exacerbated not just by more automation, encouraged by the increased safety risks of labor-intensive production, but more by the dropouts and large reduction in learning due to the suspension of in-person learning in schools and colleges that affects young people in poor families (in poor countries, the effect of the pandemic has been most damaging on the human capital of youth). While the consequences have been hard for the disadvantaged minorities and women in all countries, poor countries with scant fiscal, administrative, and health resources have suffered most.

Even as a hundred million or so of such people, by the estimates of international organizations like the World Bank (Mahler et al. 2021), got into extreme poverty in the wake of the pandemic, Bloomberg Billionaires Index data will tell you that just five of the richest billionaires of the world *added* about $340 billion to their net worth in the year 2020. Apart from owning businesses that have thrived as a result of the pandemic (like Amazon or Zoom), these billionaires have also gained from the central bank remedial policy of massive purchases of financial securities of private companies, which have boosted asset and stock prices.

Will the rising inequality and sheer scale of human suffering strengthen the redistributive demands of social democratic parties? Or, as has happened so often in the recent past, will the increasing concentration of economic and political power in the hands of oligarchs, big firms, and their lobbyists succeed in smothering redistributive efforts? The results will, of course, vary from country to country, but there is some hope in the air, at least in democratic countries. This is not simply because some of the large cash assistance programs and public health interventions tried out in the crisis may linger in modified forms. It's also because opposition to generous welfare benefits is diminishing even in rich Anglo-Saxon countries. According to the British Social Attitudes Survey for 2020, carried out by the National Center for Social Research, while 30 percent of Britons in 1987 thought welfare recipients did not deserve benefits, by 2019 this had fallen to 15 percent. In the United States there has been overwhelming popular support for President Joseph Biden's large relief-cum-stimulus package. Compared to the stinginess of measures to help the masses immediately after the financial crisis reached its height in 2008, the state response has been faster and more generous after the pandemic—mainly in rich countries, but also in many poor countries. Between February 2020 and January 2021, according to the count of the International Labour Organization (ILO), over sixteen hundred social-protection policies were launched in different parts of the world (see ILO 2021).

As I indicated in Chapter 1, more than economic inequality, economic insecurity is likely to loom large in the policy environment in many countries in the postpandemic world; workers usually are less worried about the rising income share of the top 1 percent, and more about the precariousness of their own incomes, jobs, pensions, and health care and social security benefits. Social democrats will win more support if they emphasize these areas of their traditional strength and extend their domain to include workers in the currently unprotected informal sector, as well as new kinds of insecurity like those brought about by pandemics and ecological distress.

Social democrats may also benefit from backing relatively new policies (particularly outside Europe), such as temporary wage subsidies to discourage mass layoffs. These have been tried out in the current crisis in many countries, both rich and poor, and social democrats may consider supporting their use over longer periods. These subsidies could and should replace the large capital and fuel subsidies in many countries that encourage job-replacing, capital-intensive, and energy-inefficient methods of production and transportation. Above all, social democrats would benefit from giving utmost priority to a complete overhaul of the public health system, which is broken in countries like India and the United States, as became evident in their chaotic handling of their meager public health resources during the pandemic (the mismanagement took catastrophic proportions in India's second surge of the virus). Some developed countries, like Australia, Germany (despite some fumbling at the initial vaccine rollout time), Japan, New Zealand, South Korea, and Taiwan, and even relatively poor areas with more sturdy public health infrastructure like Vietnam and the Indian state of Kerala, performed much better. Of course, with the rapid transmission of the new variants of the coronavirus the system got overloaded or collapsed in some of the countries that had had earlier successes, and the inevitable virus fatigue has dimmed their earlier spirit. With the large cuts under austerity policies of recent years, the weakened public health systems in Italy and the United Kingdom did not initially perform as well (though vaccine rollout was impressive in the latter). In the United States, vaccine rollout has been moderately successful, hampered largely by political polarization.

THE PREMIUM ON A MORE ASSERTIVE ROLE OF THE STATE

Markets are particularly ill equipped to handle the risks of pervasive catastrophic events like the pandemic. The disaster has renewed appreciation for the special role of the state in pooling and underwriting risks for masses of people. In general, market fundamentalism is now on the defensive everywhere, there is a premium on resilience over allocational efficiency, and the state is encouraged to play a more assertive role. Social democrats may give this a qualified welcome. They will surely welcome such a clear demonstration of the indispensability of the state to managing a public crisis. They will be glad that people (particularly the young) will now pay more attention to government procurement capabilities and to public investment in infrastructure, research and development, and other domestic and international public goods (like coordination on global pandemics). They will cheer the fact that macroeconomic policy makers (as well as financial markets) seem now a bit less resistant to the idea of larger fiscal deficits for the sake of relief and stimulus to the economy and sometimes also to the idea that bailouts of private companies should be conditional on restrictions on corporate payouts to managers and shareholders and on adherence to worker welfare and environmental goals.

In general, the capacity of the state to grapple with emergencies is back on the agenda in most countries and is likely to stay there as the public worries about future pandemics and other potential natural or manmade disasters. Hopefully the increased technological capacity of the state to reach out to people through digital means will be a help. As the cases of success and failure in coping with the pandemic have shown, institutional resilience, agility, preparedness, transparency, and the democratic accountability of the state are crucial. Social democrats may also be relieved that in the face of the new virus, distrust of experts and scientific reasoning, shared by populists and postmodern writers alike, has also declined somewhat. The gross mismanagement of the health crisis by populist demagogues (like Jair Bolsonaro, Boris Johnson, Narendra Modi, Vladimir Putin, and Donald Trump), who were at least initially in denial of the seriousness of the virus or who promised early victory over it, has also been widely noted.

But social democrats will also need to be careful. Under the cover of fighting the virus (say, in testing and contact tracing) the surveillance and monitoring power of the state has increased everywhere. This is a continuation of the disturbing trend toward "surveillance capitalism" sponsored or enabled by big tech with "big data" and intrusive software (being taken to an extreme by the digital totalitarianism of China). Elected authoritarian leaders in countries like Hungary, India, the Philippines, and Poland are also using the pandemic as an opportunity to overcentralize regulations, undermine or hollow out democratic institutions, and crack down on political opposition and dissent, and in countries like Brazil to roll back environmental regulations. In enforcing the lockdown, police excesses and violations of democratic accountability have been quite common. Some might argue that we should forgive such excesses in a time of crisis. And it is certainly true that decisive central coordination is necessary, particularly in mobilizing finance and technical expertise, allocating scarce medical resources (and vaccines) across regions, and aligning travel restrictions with lockdowns and openings. But such things do not require draconian measures. And the success stories in fighting the virus have often involved (as in Kerala and Taiwan) considerable decentralized decision-making, information dissemination, and vigorous participation by local officials and communities. In contrast, the overcentralized, draconian lockdown in Shanghai in March 2022 caused a great deal of unnecessary suffering and resentment.

CONFLICTING FORCES AT THE COMMUNITY LEVEL

Community-level social solidarity is a social democratic asset in fighting the pandemic, and it has been in much display recently. Researchers in Denmark's HOPE Project (a study of how democracies cope with the pandemic) show that community spirit (in Denmark, *samfundssind*) helped keep it under control, mainly without mandates or curfews (as reported in the *New York Times,* November 14, 2021). A study recently reported in the *Lancet* ("Pandemic Preparedness and COVID-19" 2022) of 177 countries for the period January 1, 2020, to September 30, 2021, estimates that if every country in the set were to be moved to the seventy-fifth percentile of trust in their fellow citizens—roughly South Korea's level—it would have prevented 40 percent of global infections.

There have been many heartwarming stories from different countries of mutual help in the community and of heroic work by essential service workers. One of the exemplary cases of community organization and participation has been in the London borough of Camden. When the pandemic started, the Camden Council mobilized resources, staff, and volunteer services to prevent hunger, support distressed businesses, protect vulnerable children and isolated adults, and ensure that young people could continue to learn at home. They quickly set up local COVID-19 testing centers and mobile vaccination units. In Taiwan, collaboration between the public sector and the civic technology community quickly developed a contact tracing system without giving up privacy protection.

But there have been opposite kinds of stories as well. Social distancing in the shadow of infection and the fear and stigma it has generated can sow suspicion of others in the community (as a character in Jean-Paul Sartre's play *No Exit* says, "Hell is other people"). We've seen neighbors distrusting neighbors and community vigilantism driving people to hide their symptoms, thus paradoxically enhancing contagion. In many Indian cities, some neighborhoods were isolated and guarded by residents so that outsiders (particularly poor people) could not enter; some health workers were banished from their old neighborhoods for fear of infection. It is possible that such social distrust is more acute in heterogeneous, unequal societies.

One may remember Daniel Defoe (1722) writing about London in the plague year of 1665, "Fear and panic could destroy the city as much as plague itself. Many of the doctors fled, along with the rich and powerful; quacks preyed on the poor. . . . Neighbors informed against each other. People lied to each other—and to themselves."

This mutual suspicion also applies to the level of the political community called the nation-state. The pandemic has amplified xenophobia, anti-immigration bias, and the blaming of other countries for spreading the virus—all of which the populist demagogues have made full use of. In some countries the paranoia has involved scapegoating domestic minority communities as "superspreaders" (for example, Muslims in India, mirroring the case of Jews in medieval plague-ridden European cities). Even in the race for the development of a vaccine against the virus there have been alarming signs of a kind of "vaccine nationalism," foreshadowing some of the mad scramble as the vaccines arrived: the rich countries, containing 15 percent of the world population, cornered half of the vaccine supply. As usual the poorest people and countries suffer the most in this. This is a global health disaster, apart from being a moral one.

All of this means that social democratic labor and civil society organizations have to take the lead in resisting pressures from communities and nations eager to race to the bottom. They must lead internationally in favor of efforts toward cooperation in issues involving global public goods from which all countries gain (like research on matters of public health and vaccine distribution, or collective attempts to prevent and mitigate climate change, cyberattacks, international terrorism, or organized crime) and to show that even in cases where there are some conflicts of interest among countries (for example, in defining global regulatory standards in labor, finance, trade, or tax havens) it is possible to come to flexible compromises in a way that the gains are shared and no country loses.

CULTURAL STRUGGLE

Yet, as we saw in Chapter 1, the struggle is often as much cultural as economic. Both on global and local matters a cultural backlash has often swamped progressive or redistributive measures that you expect the poor to demand. Social democrats have to recapture the local cultural territory appropriated by the populists and work hard at the grass roots in taming and transcending parochial nativist passions and prejudices against minorities, immigrants, and foreigners. One has to persuade people about the benefits of diversity and the contributions to national public welfare by minorities and immigrants, and the national benefits of an open economy, with appropriate social insurance against its risks.

But one also has to recognize that a more open attitude about poor workers from the ethnic *majority* communities, along with more sensitivity to their perception of social demographic threats, may go some way in assuaging their resentment about many liberal social democrats seeming to care more for minorities and immigrants. They can try to relieve some identity-based tension by making their advocacy of economic justice programs part of a common goal of humanitarian uplift and citizenship rather than a sectarian agenda of catering to some particular social groups. Balancing the interests of the aggrieved sections of the majority and chronically oppressed minorities is difficult, but doable, if approached with some finesse and openness to compromise (unions in the United States, like SEIU and UNITE HERE, have started on this). In his 2019 book *Merge Left: Fusing Race and Class, Winning Elections, and Saving America,* Ian Haney López talks about the findings of the Race-Class Narrative Project (which he cofounded in 2017) that one faces a tough tightrope act, and yet he observes how presenting issues in combined appeals to race and class was more convincing than the "dog whistle racial fear message," on the one hand, and color-blind economic welfare programs, on the other.

As I noted in Chapter 1, one also has to recognize that over the last several years right-wing populists have captured much of the social media, used it to amplify the general sense of insecurity for which they deem themselves the designated saviors, and insulated their followers in closed ideological echo chambers with such resolute adroitness that it is indeed a formidable task for social democrats to break through the walls of disinformation and conspiracy theories and earn enough general trust and legitimacy in the vicious "culture wars."

On nationalism, I discussed in Chapter 3 the case of civic nationalism, which combines pride in one's cultural distinctiveness (and maybe soccer teams) without giving up on some of the shared universal humanitarian values usually enshrined in liberal constitutions, including tolerance for diversity (as evident sometimes in the composition of those soccer teams). (A popular chant among the mostly white working-class fans of the Liverpool Football Club, roaring from the stadium their admiration for the prolific goal-scoring, devoutly Muslim, Egyptian player Mohamed Salah, goes like this: "If he scores another few / then I'll be Muslim too!") I have also discussed how in India, arguably the world's largest multinational society, the earlier social democratic view of civic nationalism based on pluralism and diversity has been challenged by the narrow Hindu-supremacist ruling right-wing party.

Social democrats have sometimes been understandably preoccupied by the historical injustice to some identity groups, alienating in the process many conservative members of the working class who feel left out. In the United States, slogans like "Defund the police"—adopted by some Black Lives Matter groups and their supporters, for all their justified rage at police brutality—have raised anxiety about crime and the law and order situation not just among the white population, but also among some minority groups, who voted for Trump, as election surveys have shown. On a related issue, Mark Lilla did not make himself popular with social justice warriors when in his 2018 book *The Once and Future Liberal* he advised young American liberals to have this sense of "compromise": "You need to visit, if only with your mind's eye, places where. . . . You'll be eating with people who give genuine thanks for dinner in prayer. Don't look down on them. As a good liberal you have learned not to do that with peasants in far-off lands; apply the lesson to Southern Pentecostals and gun owners in the mountain states. . . . Impose no puritan tests on those you would convince."

In this kind of culture war, social democrats should keep in mind that their strength ultimately lies not in fighting battles on new frontiers of identity puritanism but in finding ways of transcending the divisions of society based on identity. In labor movements one way of weakening ties to birth-based identities may be to give workers a voice in firm governance, which, as well as even a tiny stake in profit sharing, can instill a pride in where they work and what they produce. Labor organizations and related social movements, while ensuring social protection, could channel the economic anxiety of workers in the direction of solidarity in local civic engagement, democratic participation, and shared human rights, diverting them from the colorful ethnonationalist narratives that demagogues use to mobilize this anxiety. They could be sensitive to the genuine communitarian needs and the cultural neglect that workers feel in their relation to cosmopolitan liberal leaders. This may go some way in bridging the gulf between the two groups of workers that is responsible for the erosion of support of social democratic parties among blue-collar workers.

7

Social Democracy and Capitalism

A RESTRUCTURING OF THEIR FRAUGHT LINK

Different people mean different things when they talk of social democracy and its somewhat close kin, democratic socialism. I usually associate the former with the mode of production remaining essentially capitalist, though with some important modifications, and the latter with ownership or control of the means of production resting primarily with nonprivate entities (the state, cooperatives, or worker-managed enterprises). In this sense US senator Bernie Sanders and his followers wrongly describe themselves as democratic socialists; to me they are social democrats.

In social democracy those important modifications to the capitalist mode of production may involve substantial reform in the governance of firms, in the institutions of collective bargaining, and in the fiscal power of the democratic state to raise taxes to fund a significant expansion of redistributive and infrastructure programs. Yet these modifications will remain constrained by what used to be called structural dependence on private capital. How far that structural limit can be pushed will vary with a country's institutional history, political culture, and social norms. In mobilizing support, both organizational and ideological, much will depend on how far the modifications of capitalism can be shown to leave unhampered the mechanism of productivity growth and innovation, which Joseph Schumpeter considered the engine of capitalist dynamics. Is there a magic balance achievable under social democracy? This will be central to the first part of my discussion in this chapter, as I often find that my social democratic and democratic socialist friends do not pay adequate attention to the question of innovations. I shall then also comment on the need for significant reforms in the financial system, labor market policy, and election funding for a social democracy to function properly.

FIRM GOVERNANCE AND INNOVATIONS: THE WORKER'S VOICE

Social democrats often insist on a larger voice for workers in the governance of the firm. (In the 2020 US presidential primary campaign, Senator Elizabeth Warren was a main proponent of this idea.) At a time of widespread job losses, this voice can be particularly important in influencing the firm's decision to outsource or relocate. Outside the firm workers also demand antimonopoly regulations not just because corporate concentration of power is bad for an efficient economy and democratic polity but also because such concentration of buying power in the labor market (what economists call monopsony power) weakens labor's bargaining strength. Of course, issues of competition are somewhat different between product markets and labor markets—the latter are often more local than the former (increasing the market power of employers), and the latter sometimes cut across several product markets (so deconcentration in one product market may not be enough). One has to also pay attention to some provisions in the allowable labor contracts; the standard restrictions, like noncompete clauses (even at the bottom skill levels), limiting the ability of the worker to leave one firm and work for another, mainly increase the market power of employers.

Social democrats also ask for labor to play an active role in negotiations on international trade agreements, which are currently shaped by powerful corporate lobbies. Similarly, social democrats oppose unregulated financial capital and its free international mobility, as both destabilize capitalism and weaken labor's bargaining power and job security.

To all of this one may raise the objection that with all these improvements in the bargaining power of workers, social democracy must hurt the cause of technological innovations, and thus productivity growth and improvements in our standard of living. I am going to argue that this is not necessarily so. But before I do, let me mention two issues relevant here that are not central to my argument. One is that some kinds of "innovations" (particularly in the financial sector, like the cleverly repackaged mortgages used in subprime lending in the United States) that became prominent before the financial crisis of 2007–2009 are surely not worth the great devastation the crisis caused, and in any case have a minimal effect on productivity growth in the real economy. The second, on a more personal note, is that whenever I have visited Japan in the last two or three decades (the so-called lost decades of stagnation) I have come away with a sneaking feeling that, for all of the stagnation, the Japanese standard of living is reasonably comfortable, and if it can be rendered environmentally and fiscally sustainable, maybe Japan and other rich countries do not need the frantic pursuit of more and more innovations. The story is, of course, different for developing countries, where productivity and living standards are still very low. But for these countries the challenge often is not that they really require new innovations but that they need to catch up with technical changes pioneered elsewhere and adapt them to local conditions. Of course, I am not suggesting we abandon the search for innovations. Indeed, for all countries, and in a whole range of sectors (e.g., in public health or in the mitigation of environmental damage), innovations will be crucial as we go forward.

The question of technological innovations under systems that are alternatives to capitalism is important not just today; they also played some role, at least in Europe, in the evolution of social democracy. There was a time in the immediate postwar period when the workers in some western European countries were sufficiently politically powerful to have been able to democratically upend much of the capitalist system if they really wanted to and replace it with some form of democratic socialism. But astute consideration of the prospect of more innovation and productivity growth under capitalism persuaded many of their leaders that the workers' share of a larger economic pie would in the long term get them more, even at the expense of allowing a significant share of the pie to the capitalists.

But what about giving labor a larger role in firms' governance? Does it hurt innovations? Here we have some empirical evidence from Germany, where labor has long had a significant voice in governance of the firm, in the form of the *Betriebsrat* (works council) or more generally what is called codetermination or shared governance. Although codetermination exists in some other countries of continental Europe (and recently spread to Canada and South Korea), it started earliest in Germany, where worker representation on supervisory boards of large companies has reached parity with shareholder representation. These worker representatives have a significant influence on investment and financial decisions, as well as control of executives. Observational data on the German works council suggest a generally positive effect on productivity, particularly if the firm has profit sharing and collective bargaining arrangements. The works council also helps in building trustful industrial relations, in improving information channels between managers and workers, and in carrying out work toward environmental goals like emissions reduction. (Of course, trustful industrial relations are so scarce in typically hierarchical workplaces—as in, say, much of India and the United States—that one may need more social and structural changes before codetermination can even begin to work.)

Simon Jäger, Benjamin Schoefer, and Jörg Heining (2021) have gone beyond observational data and used quasi-experimental evidence on German firms to come up with some interesting findings on the effects of shared governance. They show that shared governance significantly raises firm productivity, without negative effects on profitability, capital investment, or the capacity to raise external finance. They also show that it reduces outsourcing by the firm and improves women's representation on the supervisory board. Their study also suggests that shared governance does not have any differential effect in firm exit (or facing bankruptcy) compared to other firms, which means that labor representation does not significantly block firm exit or restructuring. There is some indirect evidence that worker-elected representatives on the supervisory board of a firm can have longer horizons in matters like investment and more stake in the firm compared to the outside shareholder members of the board. This may make it easier for a firm to take up innovative projects with larger risk but higher return.

It is possible that between the two types of innovations I mentioned in Chapter 4—*disruptive* innovations (which often upend incumbent firms) and *incremental* innovations (which can be carried out even in large incumbent firms, but over time accumulate to quite a lot of productivity change)—social democratic firms may be more conducive to the latter type. In Germany, Japan, South Korea, and elsewhere the innovations are more often of the incremental kind. Even when exit of inefficient firms or plants becomes necessary for the innovation process, it may be somewhat more acceptable to workers when social democracy can arrange for universal social protection systems that delink the economic security issue from particular jobs.

FIRM GOVERNANCE AND INNOVATIONS:
MIXED OWNERSHIP

There is also considerable evidence—cited in the volume edited by Douglas L. Kruse, Richard B. Freeman, and Joseph R. Blasi (2010)—of positive productivity effects from employee stock ownership and profit sharing. Similar results are available in a large 2007 study commissioned by the Treasury Department of the British government. Studying workers in US firms with meaningful programs of shared capitalism and a supportive culture of participation, and contrasting them with workers in firms that do not have such programs, Freeman and colleagues find the former to have more loyalty to the firm and pride in their work, and a willingness to think more innovatively and make creative suggestions.

Apart from supporting a bigger role for workers in firm governance and giving them stock ownership, social democracies may also try to experiment with some mixed public and private ownership and see if that helps or hinders innovations. We do not have much hard evidence on this, but there are useful recent anecdotes, most of them from China (though China is definitely not a democracy, conclusions about the effects of mixed ownership on innovations need not depend on its authoritarianism per se). In the desperate technology race that China has launched vis-à-vis the United States there are now stories about some mixed-ownership firms doing reasonably well, benefiting both from long-term finance provided by the state and equity capital and risk initiatives from the private owner-partners. In the integrated circuits sector, for example, a mixed-ownership semiconductor company established in 2016, Yangtze Memory Technologies Corporation, is already reported to be making memory chips almost as advanced as the world's best (like those made by Samsung in South Korea). There are similar stories from state-aided and -guided Chinese private firms in artificial intelligence (AI), where in some types of AI application the United States is no longer the leader. Of course, with mixed ownership and state-aided private firms there is always the danger that the firms will become too big to fail, or too much of a state favorite to fail, which may turn them after some time into cozy rental havens, prone to "socializing" losses and "privatizing" profits. Keeping international competition open can, however, act here as a healthy disciplining factor, as the recent history of Japan, South Korea, and Taiwan suggests. It may also help in keeping such firms in track if the public governing body is well equipped and up-to-date enough to be able to negotiate and manage the contracts in what is largely uncharted territory.

Apart from aid and mixed ownership in firms, the state can sometimes play a catalytic role in the innovation process through coordination and directional guidance, shaping market expectations, creating demand through public procurement practices, and underwriting risks and making strategic initial investments. There are many examples of all of this cited in Mariana Mazzucato's *The Entrepreneurial State* (2015). As she illustratively points out, every bit of technology that makes the iPhone so "smart" was government funded: the internet, GPS, its touchscreen display, and the voice-activated virtual assistant Siri.

In discussing the role of the social democratic state or the firm in the innovation process it is also important to stress that the *pattern* of innovations may be just as important as—if not more important than—the *rate* of innovations. If workers have a strong voice in the running of a firm and also in the general polity outside it, it may be possible to redirect investment in new technology by a firm and by public authorities that conform more to social priorities—promoting labor-absorbing and labor-empowering rather than labor-replacing technology, environmental, health, and other long-run goals instead of short-term profits and monopoly rights. Even with private patents the state may buy them and put them in the public domain to accelerate future research and innovations—as, to take an early example, the French state did for the patented photographic invention of Louis Daguerre in 1839, which led to the rapid development of photographic technology.

In the more recent case of encouraging the creation of vaccine against COVID-19 by private pharmaceutical companies some states, in collaboration sometimes with global funds, had made commitments to "advance purchase" to provide effective incentives.

NORDIC SOCIAL DEMOCRACY
AND INNOVATIONS

It is worth stressing that Nordic social democracy has been quite conducive to innovations. Taking the rough country ranking estimates of
the Global Innovation Index (reported jointly by Cornell University,
INSEAD, and the World Intellectual Property Organization [WIPO]),
in 2019 Sweden ranked slightly higher than the United States, and
Finland and Denmark only slightly lower. The two most conspicuous
features of the wage determination process in Scandinavian countries are the compression of wages between high- and low-productivity
firms and industries and the confederate, rather than local, collective
setting of such wage patterns. The resultant relatively low wages in
high-productivity firms and industries, and hence higher profitability,
stimulate innovations as capitalists get to keep much of the surplus
when they invest in new technology.

Contrary to popular impression the Scandinavian economic model
is thus as much about dynamic capitalist efficiency as about equality;
this was clearly stated in the original exposition of the model by two
Swedish trade union economists, Gösta Rehn and Rudolf Meidner, presented in a report to the 1951 congress of the Swedish Confederation of
Trade Unions, and subsequently developed by various Scandinavian
academic economists including Karl Ove Moene of the University of
Oslo. Of course, these distinctive features of the Scandinavian model may
be difficult to reproduce in countries with different labor institutions
and cultural mores. In India and the United States, for example, labor
bargaining, where it exists, is much too decentralized; a confederate
mode of wage bargaining would require a major restructuring of
labor institutions. Similarly, in both countries repressing the salaries
of the high-skilled workers and managers may induce large-scale emi-
gration, to an extent that is not common in the Scandinavian sociocul-
tural context, in spite of the fact that posttax, posttransfer household

income in the top decile is much higher in Canada and the United States than in Denmark or Sweden. (These problems of social democracy in one country, when the surrounding world is different, may be akin to the problems of "socialism in one country" that Trotskyists used to worry about in the now long-gone past.)

Another productivity-raising feature of Nordic countries is their active labor market policies. Denmark, for example, spends nearly 2 percent of its gross domestic product (GDP) on retraining, and on advising and monitoring the jobless and making them more employable—a percentage figure that is many times the comparable spending in the United States and four times the average for member states of the Organisation for Co-operation and Development (OECD).

LABOR RELATIONS

Outside Nordic countries and some countries in western Europe, there has been a systematic, all-around weakening in the power of labor organizations in the past few decades that has driven a wedge between productivity growth and wage growth. As a result, the share of labor (particularly of unskilled labor) in national income is declining both in rich and poor countries. With the inexorable march of automation and labor-replacing technology, and with the growing concentration of corporate market power and the political clout of an entrenched financial oligarchy, achieving a rejuvenation of the countervailing power of labor organizations is going to be an enormously difficult task. In the past three decades competition in international trade has increased, particularly since the entry of China and eastern European countries into the trade mainstream. This has led to a reduction in the rent sharing between capital and unionized labor that had been standard in rich countries. The labor share in this diminished rent has been particularly low because capital, with its threat of going elsewhere, has retained much of its bargaining power. Additionally, workers care a great deal about some nonwage dimensions, including dignity in work, which have declined with the decline of trade unions.

While for developing countries—particularly those able to participate in the global value chain—more doors have opened for selling abroad, there have also been some structural changes in the process of global production that have worked against them. The intense cost-cutting competition among rivals in the global value chain has fragmented the bargaining power of labor. Besides, labor cost is now a dwindling part of the total costs of many products and is thus less of a decisive factor in determining patterns of trade. Especially when it comes to high-valued products, factors like advantage in logistics, branding, connectivity, infrastructure (both physical and digital), flexibility in production, credit and judicial institutions, and other current rich-country advantages are already leading in some cases to what is called reshoring. This puts unskilled labor, which is relatively abundant in most developing countries, at a disadvantage.

In spite of all of this there is scope for a social democracy to carry out a variety of improvements in the bargaining power of labor. Labor organizations may consider taking steps to move away from the decentralized wage bargaining that prevails in, say, India and the United States, and toward a more Nordic-style confederate mode. This will not merely improve their collective bargaining power but may allow them to take into account the larger macroeconomic realities so that aggregative compromises between capital and labor in line with those realities are achievable. This may be viewed as more responsible unionism in the public eye. Even sectoral, rather than firm-level, bargaining may reduce the incentive of employers to weaken labor organizations in their firms and encourage firm productivity to get more surplus at the same wage rate.

In several countries there has been a recent surge in attempts at organizing some forms of collective bargaining, particularly after the special hardships experienced by workers and their vulnerabilities exposed during the COVID-19 pandemic. Since the average age of members in old-style unions in many countries is relatively high, attempts are also being made to update the methods of labor mobilization—the latter through social media and networks that are more effective than the traditional ways of working through scattered worksites (also, as they say, "It never rains on Twitter picket lines"). In the United Kingdom, where there are some signs of union morale reviving after decades of Thatcherite depredations, one can now hear many voices of consensual unionism. New labor leaders are trying to get the demographic group of the millennial generation on board, with online petitions and by paying attention to their sometimes more fragmented and individualistic concerns. Even skilled and better-paid young workers concerned about their insecure contracts are now more receptive to unionization and labor activism.

In New Zealand, where the labor market was heavily deunionized in the 1990s, there are now new attempts at fixing bargained floors to wages and work conditions across some sectors and occupations. Even in the United States there are now some signs of revival in the union movement. (A September 2021 Gallup poll—as reported in Brenan [2021]—shows that about 68 percent of respondents now have a positive opinion about unions, the highest percentage since 1965.) The recent defeat for the widely publicized unionizing vote in the Bessemer, Alabama, warehouse of union-hostile Amazon has now induced the union movement to move its organizational effort to the industry level and to attempts to mobilize Amazon customers against the harsh labor practices at the company's warehouses. New demands are often less about wage settlements and more about the way workers are relentlessly paced by robots and monitored by algorithms. A recent settlement between Amazon and the National Labor Relations Board has enabled more unionizing activity and information programs on worker rights. More recently, the workers voting to unionize in some Starbucks outlets in upstate New York, and at an Amazon warehouse in Staten Island, have been hailed as significant symbolic victories. Such stirrings in labor organizing activity in one sector can have contagious effects in other sectors, but it will still be a long journey for organized labor to recover its strength. Progress will be particularly slow in the United States until unions are put on a level playing field with corporate employers and the latter are not allowed to get away with blocking or hindering labor organizing activity without serious punishment.

Social democracies also have to keep in mind informal workers in their labor relations policies. In rich countries, informal, unorganized labor is growing, with increasing numbers of people able to telecommute and work flexible schedules in the so-called gig economy of freelancers and independent contractors. Germany's IG Metall, Europe's largest industrial union, is now opening up for self-employed workers. The Independent Workers' Union of Great Britain is similarly trying to reach out to gig workers.

In poor countries, the number of workers in the traditional informal sector often far exceeds those in the formal sector. In India, even in the nonagricultural sector, more than 80 percent of workers are informal. As these informal workers are often self-employed, labor organizations have to be particularly sensitive to their special needs, which include credit and marketing facilities, health care and childcare, and legal and insurance services. One of the most successful organizations for informal workers in India—the Self Employed Women's Association (SEWA), a trade union with over two million women participants—specializes in providing just these facilities for participants. SEWA is also at the forefront of the fledgling movement for universal basic income in India. Similarly, there are special needs in the gig economy. Unions in Germany are, for example, trying to get more worker-friendly customer review sites for the gig workers dependent on them. In the United States some small companies are coming up to provide gig workers with affordable insurance or sick leave. In India during the

pandemic the Indian Federation of App-based Transport Workers organized drivers of ride-hailing apps and delivery workers for their
minimum rights and engaged in relief work for distressed workers.

There is also a long tradition of thinking on worker-owned or
-managed enterprises, with much of this thinking sometimes more
wishful than actualized or sustained. Of course, the largest and one of
the most sustained examples of successful cooperative in the world is
that of Mondragon Corporation, the federation of worker cooperatives
founded in 1956 in the Basque region of Spain. For smaller worker-
controlled enterprises the main economic constraints on their formation and sustenance relate to the difficulty of getting credit in the
commercial loan market and of bearing the inevitable production and
market risks. Social democratic parties and trade unions can lobby for
credit subsidy, public insurance cover, and time-bound short-term commitments for government priority in procurement from such enterprises. These solutions would be particularly helpful when a private
equity investor gives up on a low-profit but otherwise viable enterprise,
threatening massive job losses and a decline in local communities. On
a smaller scale, all over the developing world there are now many successful cases of self-help groups and women's cooperatives; large unions
could give them some cover against risks and coordination problems.

The issue of job security in the formal sector, which is of central
concern to workers, is qualitatively, even desperately, different between
rich countries (where there are significant unemployment benefits,
though these are somewhat inadequate in the United States) and poor
countries (where such benefits are minimal or nonexistent). During
the pandemic many rich countries tried out generous "furloughs" or
wage subsidies to enable firms to keep workers on the payroll. This
was also tried out in some developing countries, though with less
generous amounts. Some economists worried about this delaying
the necessary reallocation of jobs from less productive to more productive sectors, but on the whole for developing countries this is a

welcome step if their goal is to encourage the development of the formal sector.

In the postpandemic world, corporate shareholders may be persuaded with some effort that negotiating and comanaging job stability and welfare and training programs with labor organizations may be good for long-term productivity and profits. It would provide a contrast to the short-term focus of managers on their year-end bonuses and the next quarterly earnings—a myopic view that regards labor as just another disposable cost item and suggests that managers should squeeze the maximum out of it with minimum pay and benefits while brandishing the threat of job insecurity. In this process, trade unions, apart from taking a responsible role in the firm / industry themselves, can also put pressure on the big pension funds to play a more active role toward such mutually beneficial long-term goals. In other words, unions may actually help in "saving capitalism from capitalists." In volume 1 of *Capital*, Karl Marx, while discussing the nineteenth-century English Factory Acts and the opposition from businessmen to them, comments that capital needs to be protected from its own "unrestrainable passion, its werewolf hunger for surplus labor."

The current right-wing government in India took the opportunity of the pandemic to ram through new labor laws to dilute economic security of workers and their labor rights (violating in the process some of the International Labor Organization conventions to which India is a signatory). Cheered on by shortsighted capitalists and their supporters in the financial media, it is pushing the economy toward more distrust, labor unrest, and stagnation in labor productivity. This is already apparent in some of the ugly and violent factory incidents that have attracted international attention. Take the case of such a recent incident when workers ransacked Wistron's iPhone assembly factory near Bangalore. This is a factory that employed about two thousand permanent workers and seven thousand "contract workers" (without any job security and benefits), and where there is no labor union. The grievances that inflamed many workers reportedly included nonpayment or delayed payment of wages, an extension of the workday to twelve hours without much notice or consultation, and inadequate safety provisions for women workers on the night shift. The Taiwanese assembler company for Apple has admitted its faults, but this kind of backlash to unfair and arbitrary labor laws is, while unfortunate, not unexpected. Similarly, there has been substantial dilution, if not outright gutting, of workplace safety regulations, and many attribute the recent rise in industrial accidents in India to this wanton deregulation.

On the trade union front in India, one source of fragmentation of the labor movement for decades has been its capture by different national political parties with different and highly contentious party-led unions. Outsiders, who may not be even workers and who dominate these unions, often have their own political agenda to pursue rather than the day-to-day workplace concerns of labor. In order to challenge this political domination, in recent years some independent movements in new directions are discernible. For example, several independent trade unions in both the formal and informal sectors in India have come together under what is called the New Trade Union Initiative. In general, as labor organizations in many countries have their back to the wall, they also have to ally with broader social movements, rallying for labor rights as part of a general commitment to human rights and participating in civil disobedience movements when such rights are increasingly in jeopardy. Only as part of such general movements, US labor unions, for example, may be able to overcome the various restrictions on solidaristic actions under which they currently operate.

DEMOCRATIZING THE SPHERE OF CAPITAL, BOTH TANGIBLE AND INTANGIBLE

The democratic commitment of social democracy should be evident as much in economic as in political governance. I have already suggested as much in my preceding discussions of the voice of labor in the governance of the firm and in fighting for the multitude of workers in their dealing with owners. In a similar vein, democratic values underlie growing calls for antimonopoly legislation aimed at reducing the concentration of economic power, which by all accounts has been enormous in recent years.

OECD data in a 2018 report show that between 2000 and 2014 the share of total sales accounted for by the top eight firms (averaged for all industries) rose by 8 percentage points in North America and by 4 percentage points in Europe. The weighted average market share of the top four firms across all industries in the United States was 32 percent in 2017. The ten largest tech companies that dominate commerce, finance, entertainment, and communications now have a combined market capitalization of more than $10 trillion, as can be seen from Companiesmarketcap.com. Matias Covarrubias, Germán Gutiérrez, and Thomas Philippon (2019) show that in the United States, in some contrast with earlier decades, the concentration has become economically more inefficient, and associated with lower investment, higher prices, and lower productivity growth.

In the decade leading up to 2019 the five largest tech firms made over four hundred acquisitions, usually of new entrants that might grow to be potential rivals. (Similar pre-emptive acquisitions by big bio-tech companies are also quite frequent.) In India, according to data put together by Marcellus Investment consultancy, between 2010 and 2020 the share in total corporate profits of the twenty most profitable firms rose from 30 to 70 percent (without much change in the composition of those firms or their productivity).

In the United States, contrary to the prevailing view of antitrust influenced by the Chicago school, which looked primarily at the effect of monopoly on prices and consumer harm, there is a new generation of legal scholars who look at the impact of concentration on all stakeholders in the economy, including workers, producers, and citizens, not just the consumers. (These scholars are sometimes described as adherents of the neo-Brandeis movement, named after Supreme Court Justice Louis Brandeis, who had pointed to broader effects of corporate concentration.) This allows them, for example, to look at the adverse impact of the giant tech companies, even when they are reducing prices for consumers (like Amazon), or providing services at what seems like zero price (like Facebook or Google). Much recent discussion has pointed to the adverse effects of the monopsony power (i.e., the dominance in labor hiring) of large companies for workers—often through devices like noncompete agreements and wage collusion.

Social democrats should not only embrace this wider view of the importance of antimonopoly activities but should also join in a growing demand for big tech to pay back for the ownership and control of the massive amounts of private data that it is collecting from its billions of customers and using profitably (as well as demand installation of appropriate privacy protection systems and antidotes to "surveillance capitalism"). Andrew Yang, another contender in the 2020 US presidential primary campaign, had launched a campaign for tech firms to pay users a "digital dividend" for their data. Since the state may be in a better position to bargain with big tech than the numerous, often unwitting, private suppliers of the data, it would make sense for it to act on behalf of the users in return for a share in that dividend going into an earmarked public fund. (As it is, the state in countries like China and India has already gotten involved in making sure that the data from their citizens remain within the country.) The city of Barcelona has implemented a civic data trust to manage its data commons so that citizens have a greater say over data collection and the purposes for which they are used. German social democratic leader Andrea Nahler has argued for a national data trust with the aim of democratizing data capital. In general, the aim of economic democracy should be to curb the growing power not just of tangible capital but also of this kind of intangible capital.

Finance is another sector in which there is a heavy concentration of largely intangible capital. The concentrated power and excessive risk taking of financial firms allowed them to precipitate the financial crisis of 2007–2009 and the attendant worldwide devastation, and then to come out of it with relative impunity. In the United States even today just three private asset-managing firms, BlackRock, State Street Corporation, and the Vanguard Group together own about 20 percent of all firms on the Standard & Poor's 500 Index. Willingness to take on these companies is only part of the problem. Another difficulty is that digitally enabled data-driven innovations are making it hard for regulators to even keep track of the multifarious activities of fintech companies and the operational risks they involve.

In this context it has been suggested that social democrats should seriously consider a public option in the financial system. The Roosevelt Institute, a think tank in New York City, has called for a modern Reconstruction Finance Corporation (somewhat on the lines of a similar financial authority in the New Deal era) to help fund the proposed Green New Deal. Social democrats in all countries may want to redirect the pension funds of workers toward such public finance authorities that facilitate public investment in the service of social and environmental goals—projects like mass transit, affordable working-class housing, publicly available broadband, public health and sanitation, and the like.

In doing this there is, however, a lot to learn from the mistakes in handling the public option in the financial system already in use for many years in countries like India, where public banks and insurance companies have been abused far too often. Although the banks do much good work to reach out to remote, unbanked, areas, where profit-minded private banks would not have gone, politicians have used them for dud loans to crony private companies and for the parking of government debt to cover unproductive expenditures.

We need something like a holding company for the public banks to keep them at arm's length from interference by politicians; this is, of course, easier said than done. Public development banks in East Asia and Germany have a somewhat better record. For countries with mainly private banking systems it has also been suggested that if all citizens are allowed to open free bank accounts directly with a central bank, with all the usual facilities of a commercial bank account, this public option might reduce the monopoly power of the big banks, apart from making it easier to run monetary policy and fiscal stimulus programs in a crisis. John Crawford, Lev Menand, and Morgan Ricks (2021) have called for such a "FedAccount program" for the American public. Such central bank accounts for the public may soon come as part of the digital currency system that many central banks are currently exploring. In October 2020 the Bahamas launched the world's first central bank digital currency, and European Union officials are hoping to create a virtual euro by 2025.

PUBLIC FINANCE UNDER SOCIAL DEMOCRACY

In the United States (where the safety net is patchy) and in developing countries (where it is often nonexistent, particularly for the vast masses of informal workers), social democrats supporting the funding of a generous welfare state (possibly including a significant universal basic income, which I will discuss in Chapter 8) have to think about restructuring the whole public finance system. This should include streamlining the existing structure of subsidies (many of them mainly going to the rich and middle classes or taking the form of energy-inefficient fuel subsidies) and revamping the system of raising taxes on the rich—to include more progressive income taxes; wealth, capital gains, and inheritance taxes; and a reformed system of local property taxes. In the postpandemic years there may be special opportunities; as Kenneth Scheve and David Stasavage have shown in their book *Taxing the Rich*, demand for progressive tax reform usually rises after major wars or fiscal crises.

Even before the COVID-19 pandemic, public opinion had slowly being warming to the idea of change. There has been renewed interest, both in academia and the media, for programs that would substantially tax capital, turning the tax system away from its heavy dependence on the taxation of labor income and consumption. Several factors caused this. First, many people have been outraged by the grotesque rise in inequality in income and wealth over the last few decades. Thomas Piketty's book *Capital and Ideology* illustrates some of the data on this in charts that cover most regions of the world. For example, the share of the top decile of wealth-holders in private property (including real estate, business, and financial assets, net of debt) went up in the United States, from about 65 percent in 1980 to nearly 75 percent around 2010, and in India in the same period from about 45 percent to about 62 percent. (One should keep in mind that these estimates based on household surveys are likely to be underestimates, as such surveys usually undercount the ultrarich and underreport their wealth.) In the same period the rise in the wealth share for the top decile in France and the United Kingdom has been modest. For China and Russia the corresponding rise has been sharper: in China the share of the top decile went up from about 40 percent around 1995 to 67 percent around 2010, and in Russia from about 52 percent in 1993 to about 70 percent around 2010. As I have indicated in Chapter 6, in the past decade financial asset owners all over the world enjoyed large windfall gains thanks to the policy of *quantitative easing* and low interest rates pursued by monetary authorities.

At the same time, in the name of encouraging investment in a competitive globalized world, the progressiveness of tax rates on income and capital has been declining in many countries. For example, in the United States there is very favorable tax treatment on capital income (profits plus returns on financial assets or savings), and the tax rates have declined substantially in the past three decades. The marginal income tax rate on the highest income level in the United States went down, from about 70 percent in 1980 to less than 40 percent in recent years; in the United Kingdom it fell from 75 percent to about 45 percent; in France it dropped from about 70 percent to slightly above 50 percent. Studies show that such large declines in top tax rates did not have a significant effect on competitiveness or GDP; they mainly accelerated inequality. In the United States there are now some attempts to substantially raise the rate of tax on capital gains, partly to stop private equity, hedge fund managers, and partners in law firms and medical associations from disguising their wages in the form of lower-taxed capital gains.

In India in this period the marginal income tax rates not only declined sharply but both wealth and inheritance taxes were abolished. In the United States and western Europe, inheritance tax rates also declined in this period, but the marginal tax rate on the largest inheritances remained significant even in recent years (around 40 percent in the United Kingdom and the United States, somewhat higher in France, and somewhat lower in Germany). In the context of the heightened financialization of recent years, where only the very rich can invest in very-high-return financial and educational assets, leading to a class of hereditary plutocrats, it is a scandal not to have substantial inheritance taxes (and also to allow, as in the United States, the very large unrealized capital gains on assets of the rich to escape taxation at the time of inheritance). It is estimated that in the coming decade households in the United States with wealth over $5 million will collectively transfer about $15.4 trillion to the next generation.

In general, the way the inheritance taxes are designed is critical. A 2021 OECD report on inheritance taxation suggests that in recent years numerous provisions have narrowed the tax base in several countries to significantly diminish its potential. The report discusses a number of reform options that may be considered to enhance the revenue-raising potential, efficiency, and equity of inheritance, estate, and gift taxes (with these taxes preferably unified). One important finding in the report is that a recipient-based inheritance tax may be more equitable than an estate tax on the total wealth transferred by donors (which is the practice in Denmark, South Korea, the United Kingdom, and the United States).

Of course, if taxes go up, so will attempts at tax evasion. An analysis of Internal Revenue Service audit data in the United States suggests that the estate tax underreporting gap due to noncompliance is estimated to be 13 percent, which is surely an underestimate. The underreporting gap is likely to be even larger in developing countries. Yet the tax can still have a large impact. There is some survey evidence that making people aware of the large aggregate amounts of inherited wealth in the upper reaches of society and the extreme inequality of opportunity that it generates may increase public support for inheritance taxes. High tax rates on capital have the additional benefit of discouraging investment in labor-displacing automation.

Recently some scholars have proposed a reformulated structure of wealth tax, avoiding some of the design flaws of earlier attempts at wealth taxation in several countries. One factor that may have increased its feasibility is that in recent years, through the concerted efforts of some governments and nongovernmental organizations, there is now somewhat more transparency in what used to be the rather murky world of international wealth holding (the latter can be gauged from the International Monetary Fund estimate, cited in Damgaard et al (2019), that about 40 percent of the world's foreign direct investment is "phantom"—i.e., accounting fictions set up to avoid taxes). This initiative has been particularly led by the Global Forum on Transparency and Exchange of Information for Tax Purposes under the auspices of the OECD and the G20 governments. In 2019 nearly one hundred countries availed themselves of the automatic exchange of information on foreign financial assets now established between tax authorities, as mentioned in an OECD 2020 report. Digitization has also improved the tracking capacity and access to large sets of consolidated data.

Recent proposals have also suggested a rather high tax threshold, which increases the political acceptability of a wealth tax and also largely resolves the problem of liquidity that middle-income households may face in paying tax on their wealth. In general, Florian Scheuer and Joel Slemrod (2021) indicate that the somewhat disappointing experience of the old wealth tax in Europe is not directly applicable to the new proposals like those in the United States, as the design features—rate schedule, broadness of base, and enforcement provisions—are now quite different.

A Reuters / Ipsos poll in January 2020, as reported in Schneider and Kahn (2020), found that 64 percent of all respondents in the United States (and even 53 percent of Republicans) were in favor of a wealth tax. In the 2020 US presidential primary campaign, Senator Warren, backed by some academic economists, suggested a 2 percent wealth tax threshold of $50 million of net worth, and a 6 percent tax rate for net worth above $1 billion. In the United Kingdom the recently created Wealth Tax Commission has estimated that a wealth tax at the rate of even 1 percent on the top decile of wealth holders can yield revenue of more than 2 percent of GDP (net of administrative costs but not considering avoidance and evasion losses).

Such detailed estimates are not available for India, but a rough calculation by S. Subramanian (2020), using Hurun's "India Rich List 2020," suggests that a wealth tax rate of a flat 4 percent on its richest 953 families alone (0.0004 percent of India's 260 million households) can yield a revenue of a little over 1 percent of GDP. If 0.1 percent of the wealth holders are targeted, obviously much more revenue could be collected even at somewhat lower average, but progressive rates. India abolished the wealth tax in 2015 on the ostensible ground that it was not yielding much revenue relative to the administrative cost. This was not surprising in view of the large number of exemptions given to different types of assets (e.g., agricultural assets; public, charitable, and religious trusts; and gold deposit bonds); the scope of the tax was further reduced in 1993, practically limiting its coverage to mainly unproductive and idle assets. The challenges of evasion and incessant litigation (particularly on valuation issues) may be hard to eliminate, but it is certainly possible to have a new restructured wealth tax yielding significant net revenue. Besides revenue collection, a wealth tax also serves other important ends, both in terms of redistributive equity and providing an improved cross-checking database for all other forms of direct taxation.

Of course, for all countries the problem of "fiscal exile" and offshore tax havens will be a persistent obstacle for quite some time, in spite of all the improvements in exchange of financial information. International efforts at tax harmonization and coordination on financial regulations, and some restrictions on short-term capital flows, will have to be energetically pursued on a multilateral basis. It has been suggested by some that a tax on foreign financial transactions collected by individual countries might be contributed to a global environmental fund from which developing countries that usually suffer most from the flight of financial capital can borrow at a concessional rate for investment in mitigation of environmental degradation. (One has to keep in mind, of course, that in a world of digital superconnectivity there are some limits to restrictions on capital mobility and taxes on financial transactions.)

In addition to raising the tax rates, social democrats—in trying to expand the tax base (and, of course, in other labor-friendly objectives)— should also keep the goal of high level of employment as a top priority (we'll come back to this goal in Chapter 9). Northern European and other social democracies have often achieved this with active labor market policies for retraining and reskilling, wage subsidies, and with public caregiving services that enable women to participate in the workforce in large numbers.

PUBLIC FUNDING OF ELECTIONS

The "democracy" part of social democracy will remain essentially rigged as long as politicians mainly depend on large corporate donations for their increasingly expensive elections. It has been estimated that in the 2020 US elections a total of $14 billion was spent by political campaigns. It is now recognized that Tony Blair and Bill Clinton's style of social democracy, wedded to high finance, is doomed to failure, eroding both social values and democratic commitments. But the most egregious recent case of a major social democratic party crashing under the burden of corruption is that of the Partido dos Trabalhadores (PT) in Brazil. The corruption scandals clearly involved the personal greed of some PT politicians, but much of the money illicitly procured was to feed the political machine of the party, which needed large sums to fund elections and to lubricate the postelection wooing of legislators of allied parties to rally behind particular policy programs. After the big corruption scandal involving the Odebrecht construction conglomerate spilled over into several other Latin American countries, there seemed to be some moves to limit corporate donations.

In the United States the largely unregulated, and court-sanctioned, role of corporate money for campaign finance before elections and for lobbying of legislators between elections has made a mockery of democracy and the rule of law. What value does the rule of law have when laws are essentially for sale? The situation is in some respects even worse in India, where the ruling right-wing party legally raises corporate money many times greater than the total raised by all other parties combined, not to speak of what it may bring in from undocumented illegal finance. Matters have been made murkier by the con game of what is called an electoral bond (with very little disclosure requirement), introduced by the current regime under the guise of what was called electoral reform. In order to raise money, some smaller parties at election time now sell their party "tickets" for contesting elections to the largest contributors to the party fund. This is also the practice in several African countries.

In recent years some candidates in rich countries have been successful in crowd-funding or gathering small donations from numerous people. This is unlikely to work in all cases, and seldom in poor countries. Social democrats have to seriously consider the alternative of public financing of elections, with, of course, a system of strictly enforced limits on (and independent auditing of) expenditure by both parties and candidates. It is worth learning from cases of relatively successful reforms in the public funding of elections in some social democratic countries. In Canada there is significant public funding (though since 2016 it is mostly reimbursement for campaign expenses rather than direct public subsidies to parties), with stringent regulations on ceilings of election spending; there are also tax incentives for small contributors, though the tax rebates on political donations help the bigger donors more. Germany has relatively generous public funding of parties (and their associated foundations) and uses public grants that match the funds from small contributors, but there are no limits on private donations. Spain has also substantial public subsidies for parties, and limits to corporate donations. It is substantial in Belgium as well, with strict limits on election spending and private donations. In France the public funding of parties has declined over time; it is lower than in Belgium, Germany, or Spain, and there are limits on private donations. Sweden, where corporate donations used to be a major source for political parties, public subsidies are now generous enough for the parties to voluntarily stop accepting corporate donations.

In her recent book *The Price of Democracy,* Julia Cagé shows that the fight for public funding of elections has been a losing battle in many countries; but she goes on to suggest the introduction of what she calls "Democratic Equality Vouchers," whereby all taxpaying citizens can specify in their tax returns every year a certain amount of public funds that should go, anonymously, to a party or movement of their choice (the city of Seattle in the United States has a somewhat similar system for municipal elections). This is, of course, difficult or inadequate in developing countries, where only a small proportion of citizens pay income taxes. But Cagé's other suggestion of eliminating tax deductibility for (large) private political donations should be implementable in most countries.

To be viable and vigorous social democracy has to grapple with these systemic issues arising from the structural dependence of both politics and the economy on capital, by increasing the role of labor in firms' governance, influencing the pace and pattern of innovations, democratizing the financial and fiscal space, and draining the current swamp of electoral funding. This is, of course, in addition to what I have recommended in Chapter 6, where I discussed the role of social democracy in providing minimum security and social insurance in a world of increasing precariousness in the life of workers, with the state pooling and underwriting risks and worker organizations going beyond their usual bargaining roles to work at the community level to assuage various kinds of cultural insecurities.

We may also gather here the threads of the comments in preceding chapters on the somewhat ambiguous viewpoint on economic competition that may seem to characterize the social democratic approach taken here. On the one hand, this approach supports leveling the playing field and ensuring equality of opportunity for everyone. This includes attempts to curb the concentration of economic power in a few hands or firms and to encourage the building of centers of countervailing power, be they trade unions, civil society organizations, or environmental activist groups. In the increasingly important knowledge economy this also implies fewer state-assigned monopoly rights (like patents), particularly when they effectively hinder future innovations. One may also cautiously tread here on the controversial realm of global competition, where the relatively unrestricted flow of trade and participation in the global value chain (particularly of traded parts and components) may be rendered beneficial to all if the social democratic state is alert in compensating losing groups and retraining them (as it is in Nordic social democracies that are vigorously protrade).

On the other hand, we have to be careful so that competition does not turn into a race to the bottom. This is as true in competition between groups and regions within a country as in the cases of international trade, exchange rates, or tax policy. As I noted earlier in this chapter, the intense cost-cutting competition among rivals in the global value chain can fragment the bargaining power of labor or dilute environmental standards. A social democrat may generally advocate relatively unrestricted trade and global rules of competition, but may also be supportive (up to a point) of some kinds of (time-bound) domestic industrial policy that encourage particular firms or sectors, as long as the emphasis is on productivity improvement more than price distortion. I have also stressed the importance for social democracy of restrictions on international capital flows and regulations on excessive financialization, both of which can otherwise be destabilizing and hurtful to workers' economic security.

Of course, restrictions on capitalist freedom and corporate concentration in an otherwise mainly capitalist mode of production are tricky, if not recklessly bold, to implement and sustain. The oligarchic interests of business and capital that now dominate most democratic polities will not easily give up on the powers they have acquired. It is, of course, an uphill task to build cross-class political coalitions, mass organizations, social movements, and citizens' initiatives in forcefully pushing an alternative political agenda and moral narrative. New forms of technology and social media may provide powerful tools for mobilizing what seems like the already somewhat energized young people in many countries for a revamped and revitalized social democracy program. (In Taiwan a government-maintained and widely accessed digital platform named Join hosts democratic debates and tries to build consensus in many policy areas.) As I noted in Chapter 6, there is also a new appreciation all around for the need for more social spending, mitigation of environmental risks, and a more assertive role of the state in administering to these needs. One also hopes that it may be possible to persuade some sections of the business world that social democratic improvements in workers' participation, welfare, and morale within a modified framework of capitalism may not conflict with their long-term interests of productivity and profits, and that, as I have argued, capitalism can be saved from myopic capitalists.

8

In Search of Economic Security

UNIVERSAL BASIC INCOME

The COVID-19 pandemic and the associated lockdowns have had a severe impact on the world's poor. In coping with the dire economic crisis, many developing countries have resorted to cash assistance to the poor for immediate relief. Many macroeconomists have pointed out that, in addition to providing direct relief, these programs were badly needed to boost mass consumer demand in one of the deepest slumps of general economic activity in many decades. As I have been an advocate for universal basic income (UBI) in poor countries for more than a decade now—my first published paper on the subject came out in India in March 2011—I have often been asked if the widespread adoption of such cash assistance programs indicates that it is now a propitious time for UBI. In thinking about this, we should be clear that these programs, welcome as they may be, are quite different from UBI. Most are only temporary and apply only to the poor, not to everyone. I think those who like me have supported UBI have usually thought about its being established permanently to deal with the insecurities prevalent in a more "normal" state of the economy, and designed with appropriate institutions, a political support base, and administrative structures in place. Of course, I'll not object if in a postpandemic world attempts are made to help the temporary crisis programs ultimately extend or evolve into a more general UBI program in poor countries.

A BIT OF HISTORY

By now it is well known that the idea of UBI, or that of a guaranteed minimum income for everybody enabled by a public assistance program, has a long history in Western thought, going back about five hundred years to Thomas More (of *Utopia* fame) and his friend Johannes Vives. Over the years this idea has been supported (and also attacked) across the whole range of the political spectrum, by libertarians and socialists alike. On a practical level it has been tried on a large scale a few times: briefly in the early 2010s in two countries, Iran and Mongolia, and over the past four decades in one US state, Alaska. In each of these three cases the funding source has been the bounty from some natural resource (oil for Alaska and Iran, and copper for Mongolia). These experiments have not been widely duplicated, and many economists, even in cases where they are otherwise supportive, think that it would be much too expensive for the governments in rich countries to fund a UBI at a decent level. In recent years, however, new support has come from many policy activists and even businesspeople (including some among the techno-utopian entrepreneurs of Silicon Valley) who are worried about the work displacement effects of automation and artificial intelligence in the near future. Interest seems likely to rise further as the current pandemic, and others that may follow, may induce employers to avoid production conditions where lots of workers have to congregate.

In this chapter, I shall primarily talk about the possibilities for UBI in developing countries, where special factors other than looming automation may make the program imperative, and where finding resources for a reasonable UBI supplement may be within the realm of fiscal feasibility. My friend Philippe van Parijs—the Belgian political philosopher who has been one of the leading intellectual proponents of UBI over many decades and who has been a source of inspiration for me to think along these lines—once in discussing my work made an interesting observation about where UBI on a large scale might get its start. He said that just as Karl Marx had originally thought that the communist revolution would first come to an industrially developed country, but it actually came to relatively poor countries, maybe UBI, even though originally thought up for rich countries, would end up coming first to a poor country.

UBI IS NOT NECESSARILY VIEWED
AS AN ANTIPOVERTY PROGRAM

Let me start by pointing out that I have noticed an important difference in emphasis between my position on UBI and that of many of my fellow development economists. The latter look upon UBI (or a UBI supplement) as part of an antipoverty program; some think of it as an administratively simpler substitute for other antipoverty programs, while others think of it as supplementary to those programs. Then they have to contend with other, more skeptical, development economists who try to show that UBI is less cost-effective in reaching the poor than more targeted antipoverty programs. Paying the rich in order to better reach the poor is not always an overwhelmingly persuasive argument.

In the implementation of antipoverty programs there are usually *exclusion errors* (some poor people are missed) and *inclusion errors* (some not-so-poor people are included). These errors can be quite large, particularly when means testing is difficult to implement. For example, in India, where targeted programs used something like a below the poverty line (BPL) card to mark the eligibility of the poor, some survey data have shown that, through administrative lapses and malfeasance, about half of the poor people do not have the BPL card, while about one-third of the nonpoor do.

By design, UBI includes all people and excludes none. To those who look to UBI as mainly an antipoverty device, it is worth the "mistake" of inclusion if the result is that no poor people are left out. Sometimes they suggest some easily enforceable ways of reducing the inclusion error—for example, by denying the UBI to the small, easily traceable fraction of people in a poor country who own cars or pay income tax. In any case, it is easier to weed out the few rich than to search for the really poor among the vast numbers who are almost poor. To the supporters of targeted policies, however, the inclusion error is too large and tends to make UBI too costly a means of reaching the poor. Of course, the magnitude of these errors will vary from context to context, and so it may be difficult to generalize for or against these two different positions among the poverty fighters.

At this point, before I describe my own approach to UBI, I should note that a UBI policy is different from a guaranteed minimum income policy, where the government simply tops up a household's income when it falls below a prespecified minimum income level. While this approach may be less expensive than a UBI supplement, it may be difficult to implement in poor countries, where we have very little data on household income (particularly where the self-employed in the informal sector do not have accounts or documents of income earned), and also because it provides incentives for people to understate their income. It also gives employers with market power the incentive to underpay workers.

It is also worth noting a finding of various small-scale experiments with UBI started by some city mayors in the United States. Researchers note that the universality of the programs largely attenuates the stigma associated with targeted "dole" recipients. They also note that as an antipoverty program, UBI wins more support from the middle classes, who also benefit from it, than do targeted programs that leave out the middle classes. Targeted programs sometimes make the middle classes reduce their stake in public services and their trust in government, while more widely based, nearly universal programs increase trust between all citizens and the state and also raise the revenue to gross domestic product (GDP) ratio, as happened in the last decade in Nepal (similar evidence is also available from South Africa). We should also recall that poverty is not a static demographic category. People— sometimes the same people—move in and out of poverty all the time, which is difficult to track for official targeted programs that usually work with prefixed poverty lines and BPL cards, a problem avoided by UBI. It is also the case, of course, that many people who are just above the poverty line and might be excluded by targeted programs also re- quire a great deal of economic support (more on this below).

MINIMUM ECONOMIC SECURITY AS
THE MAIN RATIONALE FOR UBI

In my own approach to UBI, while I understand its possible use as a tool for fighting poverty, I think it has a more basic justification. I look upon it as part of a basic human right of every citizen to minimum eco- nomic security. One should remember that a right to social security was part of the United Nations Universal Declaration of Human Rights of 1948 (in articles 22 and 24). In recent years, even in rich countries, such security has been in short supply. Globalization, automation, the decline in labor institutions, the expansion of the so-called gig economy (where jobs and incomes are unstable or uncertain), and cuts in public services under macroeconomic austerity policies have made the life of ordinary workers more precarious, causing them a great deal of stress and anxiety. And then the pandemic and the associated lockdowns heightened the sense of social insecurity even further, particularly in countries (like India or the United States) without a robust public health infrastructure.

In developing countries, the social safety net is usually even patchier than in the United States. Policy makers in these countries have long been preoccupied with poverty reduction, and most developing countries have made considerable progress in this respect over the past few decades, at least up to the onset of the pandemic. But large fractions of the population, who may be technically above the poverty line (which in poor countries is usually a line of extreme destitution), suffer from all kinds of brutal risks in their daily life and livelihood. These include weather fluctuations that affect agriculture (now likely to be increasing in severity with climate change), job losses, illnesses in the family or among animals used in production, or pest infestation. A basic income floor would provide partial insurance against such risks without the administrative costs of checking for the usual problems of moral hazard and adverse selection that commercial insurance projects involve. In trying to expand the domain of UBI much beyond the poor, I am more concerned about these highly insecure, numerically large, sections of the population and less bothered about the inclusion error that people with the targeted antipoverty approach worry about.

When I am asked to justify why UBI should be given even to the plutocrats, my answer is that they are entitled to it as part of their citizens' rights. Just as we recognize the right of plutocrats for police protection against crime—a matter of physical security—as a basic right, even though they can very much afford their own private protection services, we should not deny them the right to minimum economic security in the form of a basic income. If they decide to waive it, or if some asset threshold—car ownership, say, or a threshold in income tax—can be *transparently* implemented to exclude them, I'll not object; that is on pragmatic or political expediency grounds, without yielding on the basic rights issue. In any case, some of the UBI paid to them would come back to the government in the form of taxes. As all of this implies, I look at UBI primarily as a means of relieving economic insecurity, not economic inequality. It would, however, reduce inequality, and indeed, I am going to suggest that a UBI in poor countries be funded largely by reducing currently regressive subsidies and taxing the rich, a move that would have some egalitarian consequences. In that sense it would be like the Social Security program in the United States, a universal program to relieve economic insecurity for the old that, because of the way it is funded and implemented, has a progressive net impact.

Looking at UBI from the point of view of economic security has also important implications for the labor market. In India, as in some European and Latin American countries, there exist some protective labor laws which make labor layoffs in large factories difficult even when market conditions warrant a drop in labor demand. Many business leaders and pro-business economists say this makes employers think twice before hiring and thus ultimately hurts the employment of new workers. Most trade unions, however, are avid supporters of such labor laws for ensuring job security—particularly in developing countries where unemployment benefits are nonexistent or highly inadequate. This has been a source of political tension between capital and labor. UBI can relieve some of that tension by disentangling the issue of the *security of a particular job* from that of ensuring general economic security for all workers. If everybody is entitled to a decent UBI, then losing a particular job is less traumatic for the worker.

SPECIAL FACTORS IN DEVELOPING COUNTRIES JUSTIFYING UBI

Achieving minimum economic security may be the main rationale for UBI in developing countries, but there are also some special factors that reinforce the rationale for adopting it:

- In some developing countries (particularly in North Africa and South and West Asia) the majority of women do not participate in the income-earning labor force (in India, the proportion of such adult women is more than 75 percent), as they are mostly in unpaid domestic and caregiving work. A UBI deposited in their accounts every month could go a long way in boosting their existing low autonomy and status within their families and activating their agency.

- In developing countries, some occupations are often particularly stigmatized, including manual scavenging, garbage collecting, sewer cleaning, and sex work. People usually work in these occupations because they have no other alternatives. UBI can provide them an escape ladder so that they have more choice in the labor market. It may also induce society to mechanize some undesirable but necessary jobs. Even beyond socially stigmatized work, UBI could be a great relief for the stark uncertainties in livelihood faced daily by the vast numbers of the self-employed and by marginalized casual and migrant workers, helping them to seek better jobs and more profitable investment. It would also enhance their bargaining power against the traders, middlemen, contractors, employers, creditors, and landlords they encounter.

- UBI can play a role in mitigating the incidence of clientelism in poor countries. The politics of redistribution is often centered around patronage distribution to particular groups or individuals—like job reservations, "jobs for the boys" (what the Italians call *lottizzazione*), and the disbursement of subsidized private goods such as food, fuel, fertilizers, and credit. This distorts the nature of democracy and diverts policy emphasis away from public goods, which can improve productivity and benefit everybody. In this context a universal policy like UBI can have a special social-transformative appeal, particularly if normatively one thinks of it as part of minimum citizenship rights, replacing clientelistic favors dispensed by politicians.

- Unlike in rich countries, a large fraction of workers in poor countries (sometimes a majority of them) work in the informal sector. One reason the labor movement is weak in those countries, and thus their bargaining power is low, is because the movement is fragmented by this formal-informal division. Trade unions give leadership to workers in the formal sector and agitate or lobby for wage demands and labor laws that largely protect only them. Informal workers do not enjoy the pensions and benefits of formal workers, and thus they'd benefit a great deal from UBI. To unite the labor movement one needs platforms that will benefit both types of workers. A collective demand for UBI, as with other universal benefits like universal health care, can serve as a bridge between the two types of workers and strengthen the labor movement.

ARGUMENTS AGAINST UBI

The idea of UBI often faces four general kinds of opposition at the policy level:

(1) opposition from many common people, particularly those with strong work ethic, as well as some paternalistic leaders, who argue that UBI will encourage laziness, an attitude of taking from society but giving nothing in return, and an inclination among some recipients to blow it all on drugs and alcohol

(2)   opposition from fiscal bureaucrats and conservative econ-
      omists, who think that it may break the budget

(3)   opposition from social activists who regard this as a ploy to
      undermine existing welfare programs, particularly those
      that are working reasonably well

(4)   opposition from many that any extra money should better
      be spent on education, health, and infrastructure, which
      are seriously deficient in poor countries

Let us examine these issues one by one.

To start with, the argument that UBI is an incentive to indulge in
indolence may be used against any program designed to improve the
income of the poor. In any case, the evidence that this would happen is
not strong. In recent years there have been quite a few experimental
studies on the effects of cash transfers to people in developing countries (the largest and the longest-lasting one has been the ongoing study
in forty villages in Kenya by the GiveDirectly program). Although
we still do not have evidence on the effects of permanent and really
universal income transfers or on community-level, as opposed to
individual-level, impact, there is no systematic evidence that cash transfers discourage work or encourage the use of drugs or alcohol. On
work incentives, if anything, a number of experimental studies show a
positive, though small, effect. Sometimes a UBI enables a worker to
leave a part-time or unsatisfactory job, to get internship or training, and
then get a better, full-time job. In some cases the assurance of UBI may
encourage people to take some risks and do entrepreneurial work instead of wage labor.

In addition, my own view on the possible work disincentive effect is
that, if anything, the poor are often overworked in backbreaking, oppressive work, and it will be better if they—particularly women—can
work a little less. It is possible that in some cases women who are assured
of UBI may devote more time to their caregiving work in the household.

As for taking something from society, and not giving back, if this is a major concern, it has been suggested that even though UBI is technically unconditional, one may try to develop a social norm according to which every recipient is expected to give something back to society to the best of her ability (e.g., in terms of some social service).

The financial viability of UBI is surely a major—and sometimes a decisive—issue. Much, of course, depends on how generous the amount of UBI envisaged is. In rich countries most decent sums proposed for UBI have been thought to be unaffordable or infeasible in view of what the taxpayers are prepared to bear unless the existing welfare state is substantially restructured. It is my intention to show here that, at least for poor countries, a decent UBI supplement, by the standards of those countries, may not be out of bounds of fiscal feasibility.

In 2017 a report of the International Monetary Fund estimated the gross fiscal cost of UBI (as percentage of GDP) for six countries calibrated at one-fourth of the median income per capita of each country. In general, the percentage was higher for the United States (6.4 percent), Poland (4.9 percent), and Brazil (4.6 percent) than for Mexico (3.7 percent), Egypt (3.5 percent) or South Africa (2.3 percent). But this study did not go into the question of how the UBI would be financed and how the form of financing may affect the fiscal cost itself.

FISCAL ARITHMETIC FOR AN ILLUSTRATIVE UBI SUPPLEMENT IN INDIA

I shall now present, as an example, some rough estimates that I have made over the years for a lower-middle-income country, India. I first look at the mobilizable fiscal resources in India, and then discuss how much of these can go toward funding a UBI supplement.

For many decades central and state governments in India have both been providing substantial subsidies to different sections of the population. Some of these subsidies—like those for food, education, health, water supply, sanitation, housing, and urban development—serve essential needs, often (though not always) for the common people, and so are deemed *merit subsidies*. But a majority of the subsidies happen to be for other purposes, primarily going to the better-off sections of the population, and have been called *nonmerit subsidies*. It has been estimated by Sudipto Mundle and Satadru Sikdar (2019) that the total nonmerit subsidies (both explicit and implicit) of the central and state governments together came to about 5.7 percent of GDP in 2015–2016.

On top of this, in the central budget alone, what are called revenues foregone (tax exemptions and concessions mainly to business) come to about 5 percent of GDP. Some of these concessions may be indispensable (e.g., in the case of customs duty exemptions for reexports), and some others may be less so (e.g., tax exemptions for encouraging investment in special economic zones are on the sometimes dubious presumption that without these exemptions this investment would not have taken place elsewhere anyway). It is probably not too unreasonable to take one-half of this total (i.e., 2.5 percent of GDP) as potentially available for more worthwhile purposes. Additionally, this does not count the revenues foregone in state government budgets, for which we do not have good estimates.

There is also considerable scope for fresh taxes. The tax to GDP ratio in India is substantially lower than in Brazil, China, and some developing countries. It has also been pointed out by Devesh Kapur (2020) that India's tax mobilization effort is substantially below what one expects in democracies (which typically tax and spend more than similar nondemocracies). Additionally, for all the substantial economic growth and rise in inequality over the past three decades, the tax to GDP ratio has not increased commensurately. India's real estate and property tax assessments are absurdly low compared to their market value. It has also zero taxation of wealth and inheritance and of agricultural income. This is at a time when household survey data (which usually underestimate inequality) suggest that India's wealth inequality is mounting and now almost in the Latin American range. We can roughly estimate 1.8 percent of GDP in the form of additional taxation.

All combined, there is thus a *potential* for mobilizing about 10 percent of GDP. Of course, there are several important claims on any extra resources mobilized. In particular, the needs for additional spending on health, education, and infrastructure are urgent. (Even with the most generous basic income supplement, people will not by themselves spend enough on their health and education needs, and there are public welfare reasons why the state needs to invest in all these three items.) Even keeping this in mind and allowing for an equal division of the extra 10 percent of GDP thus mobilized on these three items plus UBI, it is possible to get resources for UBI to about 2.5 percent of GDP. This very roughly implies a UBI of about Rs. 20,000 per family (or Rs. 4,000 per individual), which is a decent UBI supplement in the Indian context: it comes to about 15 percent of the average consumer expenditure in the household. (One could add to the mobilizable potential if in the post-pandemic context it is possible to raise a "coronavirus levy" that may go toward an overhaul of the public health system, which has been found to be seriously deficient in the crisis.)

We now have some relevant answers to those who think UBI would undermine existing welfare programs or take money that could be spent in better ways for the poor. The aforementioned fiscal scheme keeps the existing welfare programs untouched. (Some of these programs may be wasteful, and if they are pruned or replaced, the resource potential can even exceed 10 percent of GDP.) Similarly, in the scheme, the total 10 percent of GDP gets equally allocated among health, education, infrastructure, and UBI, so that should go some way in answering those who plead for spending elsewhere. If the social consensus is in favor of spending somewhat more in effective investment for health, education, or infrastructure, and somewhat less for UBI, I'll not seriously object.

SOME IMPLEMENTATION ISSUES

Politically savvy people will immediately point out that elimination of long-standing subsidies and the imposition of new taxes will meet a lot of resistance from many quarters and will be politically difficult to carry out. While that is true, a crisis situation like that of recent years sometimes may help soften up the resistance somewhat (particularly as inequalities and thus the taxable capacity of the rich have gone up in these years). It may thus be an opportune time to try big changes. If for some time the whole of the 10 percent of GDP is difficult to mobilize, even with half the amount one can start a UBI supplement only for women.

There are, of course, many other objections raised to the UBI proposal: about the level of UBI supplement (considered too low by some, too high by others); that it should be indexed to the cost of living so that it does not get eroded as prices rise; or that many people do not have ready access to a bank account where the UBI supplement can be easily deposited. These are mostly problems of implementation; once the idea of UBI is accepted at the conceptual and the broad policy direction levels, there can be pragmatic and flexible ways of handling such issues.

For example, some have suggested that the UBI should be a share of the GDP rather than an absolute amount. Then, even starting with a low absolute amount, with sufficient GDP growth one could soon provide a decent amount of basic income. This would also get around the issue of indexation, as the absolute amount of UBI would rise with price rises raising the nominal GDP. One practical problem with the GDP share idea, though, is that it becomes a bit murky at the political level: most common people will not have a clear idea of what GDP is and will not know what to expect as UBI, and even economists will dispute particular measures of GDP (as they have done with the official GDP measures in India in recent years).

The problem that people do not have bank accounts is serious in many countries. The general estimate is that two-thirds of people in low-income countries, and 42 percent in lower middle-income countries, do not have access to a bank account. One thus has to make do with other alternative ways of making cash payments in unbanked and remote-access areas—roving banking agents or cell phone banking have been used in some countries. Many people in some countries— more than 70 percent in Nigeria, for example—do not have any government-registered identification card (this is much less of a problem in India or Indonesia). Therefore, at the implementation level different developing countries will clearly be at different stages of preparation for the implementation of a UBI.

Over the past decade and a half the world has been subject to many traumatic events—the financial crisis of 2007–2009, stringent austerity policies, a deep slump in many economies, large-scale job losses, technological disruptions, creeping authoritarianism and ethnonationalist excesses, the increasing incidence of natural disasters (probably attributable to ongoing climate change), agro-ecological distress, mass dislocations, and a whole sequence of epidemics, the coronavirus being the latest. All of this has dangerously exposed the fragility and insecurity of the lives and livelihoods of billions of ordinary people. This has been particularly acute in developing countries, where numerous people live a hand-to-mouth existence even in the best of times, with very little in the form of social insurance. A universal basic income supplement can provide some minimum economic security in those countries, which even under the pressing fiscal constraints may not be unaffordable.

9

In Search of Security

OTHER POLICIES

In this chapter we'll briefly examine a selective set of other policies aimed at relieving economic and cultural insecurity, collecting and adding to some of the policy ideas presented in the preceding chapters.

A Gallup global survey conducted from July 2020 to March 2021 found that globally 41 percent of workers in the poorest income quintile said they had lost their job or business as a result of the COVID-19 pandemic (the corresponding number in the richest quintile was 23 percent). But long before the devastation that was wrought by the pandemic in jobs and incomes, particularly in small and informal business, the specter of vanishing or inadequate jobs had been haunting the whole world, from the blighted cities of the US Rust Belt, to the teeming cities and small towns of Central America, East Africa, or North India. The employment rate for young people in member countries of the Organisation for Economic Co-operation and Development (OECD), even just before the pandemic, was far below what it was before the financial crisis of 2007–2009. Unemployment has been a particularly distressing, and potentially explosive, problem for young people in the burgeoning population of developing countries. In Africa, for example, about 60 percent of the unemployed are young, according to International Labor Organization (ILO) data (see ILO n.d.). Youth unemployment was a major issue in the largely unsuccessful movement called the Arab Spring, and in Tunisia, the first country to lead the movement, the youth unemployment rate continues to be high (about 37 percent in 2020, the tenth anniversary of the Arab Spring), by the same ILO data. In India, according to National Statistical Office data (put out in 2021), the unemployment rate (which does not count those who had given up looking for work and opted out of the labor force) among those fifteen to thirty-four years of age was 28.5 percent in 2017–2018. In 2018, the Indian railway system announced a large recruitment drive for the most menial positions in its hierarchy—helper, porter, cleaner, gateman, track maintainer, and assistant switchman. For sixty-three thousand such positions announced there were nineteen million applicants; most of them were college students or graduates, and some even had postgraduate degrees. Even in booming China jobs are so scarce that many millions of young people are trying to overqualify themselves through higher and higher education just to have a better grasp in their search for elusive jobs.

Of course, many of these young people are looking for "good" jobs in the formal sector, with better pay and benefits and with some stability of tenure and well-defined career paths. All over the world such jobs are, in general, extremely scarce in relation to their demand (some cases of tightness in the current postpandemic labor market in rich countries notwithstanding).

"GOOD" JOBS, "GREEN" JOBS

There was a time when the essential process of development was thought to consist of a structural transformation of the economy such that people could move from the low-productivity, often backbreaking, jobs in agriculture and other traditional work of the informal sector to better jobs in the manufacturing and service sectors. In the last three decades of the twentieth century this kind of structural transformation was reasonably successful in East Asia, providing millions of formal-sector manufacturing jobs to rural migrants. This has been, however, much less successful in East Africa and India, where most of the low-skill entrants to the labor force have crowded the low-productivity informal sector. In Ethiopia some large firms showed marked improvement in manufacturing productivity, but that did little to increase employment. Indian success stories have largely been in the relatively high-skill sectors of business services and software, pharmaceuticals, and automobiles. In developing countries—for instance, Costa Rica or Vietnam, where education and training substantially improved the skill level of workers and where the infrastructure (roads, power, and connectivity) is reasonably good—jobs have expanded and small firms in supplier relationships with the formal sector have been pulled up. Otherwise, in large parts of sub-Saharan Africa, the Andes in South America, or India, there are only small islands of successful firms with relatively high productivity surrounded by a vast ocean of tiny and unproductive firms where workers who have nowhere else to go are scrounging around.

This duality in the economy has been increasing with global competition, as new technologies put a higher premium on skills and capital investment. Interestingly, this duality, which has been a persistent feature in the formal versus informal firm structure of developing countries, is now a noticeable feature of some advanced industrial countries as well. In his 2017 book *The Vanishing Middle Class: Prejudice and Power in a Dual Economy,* Peter Temin evocatively describes how the duality of employment opportunities in the American economy gets layered into the history of racial politics to perpetuate the rich and poor class divide as the middle vanishes. The recent emergence of the so-called gig economy, with work that is associated with few benefits and little security, has also expanded the informal sector in industrially advanced countries.

What is to be done? Let us briefly examine some relevant policies, which may be of varying importance and feasibility in different and changing contexts.

Since low skill levels are a major constraint both for individuals and economies, at least over the medium term, a mass program of skill formation and continuous learning for adaptation to changing technology is clearly necessary. Education programs in developing countries, unfortunately, are more often based on general-purpose rote learning that makes many high school graduates seriously unemployable, and training is costly for an individual firm, especially where there is a threat of poaching by rival firms. This is not to speak of the large problem of high school dropout rates that afflict poor countries, where young people often need to work to help their families and do not have access to scholarships or facilities for remedial learning (when they fall behind) that might allow them to balance education with family responsibilities. Vocational programs with sustained training in useful skills linked with apprenticeships in firms are, sadly, rare. This is unfortunate given how promising they seem to be. The German program, a successful example for many decades, involves potential employers contributing to funding a vocational program into which school graduates stream, connect up with potential job seekers in identified varieties of skill categories, which reduces employers' screening costs. The California community college cum vocational system, which works in partnership with local firms, has also been a useful example. There is also evidence of significant positive effects of subsidized in-firm training; for example, a study of a large firm-provided training program in Portugal, supported by the European Social Fund, shows significant positive effects on firm sales, employment, and productivity. Of course, the positive effects of general vocational programs are more broadly based than firm-specific training—sectoral training programs, on the efficacy of which there is quite a bit of evidence, provide a good compromise between the two.

During the pandemic and lockdown crises many countries, rich and poor, have turned to policies like temporary wage subsidies to discourage mass layoffs. These—rarely tried before, outside Europe—may now be added to the social democrats' policy armory for longer durations. As I mentioned in Chapter 6, these kinds of subsidies could replace the large capital and fuel subsidies in many countries that encourage job-replacing capital-intensive and energy-inefficient methods of production and transportation. One objection to such wage subsidies is than they tend to keep people tied to possibly unviable firms longer than is desirable. Thus, the more general, non-firm-specific active labor market policies and training to improve the adaptability of workers to changing demand for skills, which are associated with social democracies in Europe, may be preferable. But wage subsidies may be still defensible for the purpose of saving some small businesses in a given area (where enterprising locals are self-employed). This serves "place-based" goals, like holding up local community life, over and above just saving wage workers. Other forms of incentives, like tax credits for firms in return for specific commitments to job creation, can also be considered.

In recent years different countries have experimented with other programs to create and support training and jobs, suggesting lessons for others. In Europe there are some job guarantee programs targeted at young people—for example, since 2013 the European Union (EU) has had a program to subsidize private employment to ensure that everyone under the age of twenty-five gets training or a job. There was an earlier program in the United Kingdom, the Future Jobs Fund of 2009–2011, that funded businesses to create jobs and paid for training opportunities for unemployed young people, which was generally found to have been effective. Belgium now has a popular job voucher program in the domestic service sector (about 70 percent of the cost is borne by the government), and the evidence suggests that it has successfully increased the employment rate of low- and medium-skilled women. Even in the United States there has been talk about experimenting with government-guaranteed job programs, and the idea is popular with the general public. A November 2020 Gallup survey—Gallup (2020)—found that 93 percent of respondents (and even 87 percent of Republican respondents) supported government intervention to provide work opportunities for those who lost their jobs during the pandemic, and most of them preferred government-created jobs to the provision of more generous unemployment benefits. Of course, government guarantees of good jobs can disrupt and distort labor markets. A 2010 review of research on the effectiveness of labor market policies by David Card, Jochen Kluve, and Andrea Weber concluded that programs that improve worker skills do best, while public-sector employment subsidies tend to have, at best, a small impact for workers.

The world's largest program of government-guaranteed jobs is India's program on rural public works, which for all its "leakages" (and many cases of "unmet demand") has worked reasonably well to provide low-level rural construction jobs in agricultural lean seasons as some relief to poverty; but this is more like government jobs as last resort; these are not the "good jobs" that most workers hope for. Another program on a grand scale, suggested for both rich and poor countries, is that of starting a national public service program for young people—a kind of domestic peace corps—for a few years in various civic and public welfare programs. Some have pointed to a bonus social benefit of such a program in highly polarized societies—that of an opportunity to meet people of different backgrounds and opinions.

A rather different and a much-debated approach to improving the quality of jobs is to set or adjust a minimum wage. If the level of this wage is not set too high relative to the median wage in an area, it may sometimes facilitate the exit of low-productivity firms and push the labor market to create more "good" jobs. When an employer has buying power in the labor market (so-called monopsony power), minimum wage may even have positive effects on output and employment. A small increase in a preexisting minimum wage often brings about only a relatively small reallocation of the "rent" that the employer enjoys in the labor market to the workers, without a fall in employment. But policy makers need to be careful. In poor countries, and in poor areas of rich countries, a minimum wage set relatively high can dislocate jobs. It is also worth mentioning that in poor countries minimum wage laws are frequently violated with impunity in the private sector. Yet as an effective redistributive measure minimum wages can relieve the demand constraint in a slumping economy and also encourage women to participate in significant numbers, as they have done in the rural employment guarantee scheme in India, a country where their participation in the labor force is abysmally low.

In many situations public encouragement of union activity may be part of a "good" job policy, as unions not merely collectively fight against violations of minimum wage laws but also fight for some non-wage dimensions of work (like "dignity") which are an essential attribute of good jobs from the worker's point of view.

Beyond the labor market there may also be a case for direct government involvement in other ways. In the waves of bankruptcy that small firms have suffered in the recent crises, the government may make it a part of the loan restructuring policy to include provision for converting some of the loans from public institutions into equity stakes. One also needs—and particularly for the small business sector—customized public extension services to improve technology, management, and marketing apart from much larger public investment in infrastructure (including social housing) and connectivity on which there is a general consensus in both rich and poor countries. In view of the large heterogeneity among the small-business people in poor countries (many of them are there because they have nowhere else to go), it may be necessary to target some of the firm-level assistance to a small number of them sorted out by tests of entrepreneurial talent, and then link up the rest as the former succeed and are able to pull up some of the rest as possible employees and suppliers.

In general, given the large *social* ramifications of substantial job losses in a given area (in terms of their consequences for social breakdowns, the blighting of community life, and decline of trust in democratic values, apart from individual income losses in a directly affected industry and in associated service sector that is indirectly affected), a large and active involvement on the part of the state may be called for. Too many countries have allowed their public-sector capabilities to decay and public institutions to be hollowed out under policies of austerity, privatization, and outsourcing. What is called for is a reinvigorated program of public and private collaboration in which the state provides some leadership, long-term vision and directional guidance, initial pump-priming of risk capital to mobilize private initiative and ingenuity, and sharing of risk and reward in large projects of productive job creation.

In the related sphere of industrial policy to speed up economic growth there have been, of course, many cases of success and failure. One has to pay close attention to the particular institutional combinations of domestic political coalitions, and market structure and the policy designs that make the difference between success and failure, as well as consider the various rigorous empirical and experimental studies that have sought to discern the link between policy and outcome. In East Asia successful industrial policy has often mainly helped large firms (particularly in Japan and South Korea), but for creating jobs the focus of industrial policy has to be on small- and medium-scale firms (including those in the service sector). Ann Harrison and Andrés Rodríguez-Clare (2010) have recommended a whole range of "soft" industrial policies, not incompatible with World Trade Organization (WTO) regulations—like encouraging research and development (R&D), extension services, vocational training, supporting collective action for self-help in business clusters, improving regulations and infrastructure, among other policies—where the goal is to develop domestic policies of coordination that improve productivity more than intervene to distort prices. As I noted in Chapter 3, Philippe Aghion and colleagues (2015) cite panel data from medium- and large-size Chinese enterprises for the period 1998–2007 to show that industrial policies targeted to competitive sectors or to fostering competition increase productivity growth.

More than the centralized state coordinating such industrial policy, it is the involvement of the local governments (e.g., at the district, county, or municipal levels) that is necessary in a well-designed policy scheme of good jobs so that the local people can "own" the policy. But, unfortunately, the local governments in many countries do not have the requisite finance or technical capacity to start or follow through on policies. Yet they are more likely to have the local information and initiative to coordinate with the local labor market, involving vocational programs and local firms and their supply-chain partners. This is where investment in capacity building and public extension services are imperative, along with financial devolution and supporting infrastructure and connectivity, and public procurement policies to encourage the micro firms to merge and scale up.

Finally, the polices to improve and sustain jobs have to be integrated with a more general "green" structural transformation policy to address looming environmental problems. In their contribution to the 2017 United Nations (UN) publication *Green Industrial Policy,* Tilman Altenburg and Dani Rodrik cite examples of many new green products and service opportunities for rich and poor countries alike that have a great deal of job-creating potential. For both sets of countries these include renewable energy technologies (solar, wind, and geothermal power), both in generation and storage. Rich countries may focus on the production of electric vehicles and bioplastics, on carbon capture and storage, and on design and operation of smart grid and road pricing. And poor countries may focus on decentralized miniature electric grids, technologies of drip irrigation and rainfall harvesting, the reinforcement of sea walls, and natural-gas-powered three-wheeler public transportation.

In recent years there has been some enthusiasm in the United States for the proposal of massive public investment in green jobs under a so-called Green New Deal (although projects from the administration of President Joseph Biden fall far short of it). The European Commission has also come out with a proposal for a European Green Deal, and one hears also about a Korean Green Deal. There is much to commend in these proposals, particularly in terms of environmental and intergenerational social justice. There are also proposals in the matter of raising finance for chartering a green bond ratings agency staffed by independent experts. Danny Cullenward and David Victor (2020) suggest in *Making Climate Policy Work* that instead of attempting a contentious grand bargain, the key is to find coalitions of the willing and drive change sector by sector; a recent example is the announced deal between the EU and the United States on steel and aluminum.

On the other hand, these proposals also have some risks and deficiencies. There is always the lurking possibility of political capture by different domestic lobbying groups. Most of the proposals are particularly deficient from the point of view of global justice. For example, while proposals for global carbon pricing may be worthwhile, there is hardly any consideration in most of these proposals of the concrete steps rich countries ought to take to help poor countries so that the programs of global decarbonization become effective.

Consider the relevant history. Rich countries, those that industrialized first, have been polluting the planet for many generations. More recently, as "dirty" manufacturing has shifted to developing countries, rich countries' consumption pattern now generates much of the pollution elsewhere. Should poor countries bear the full burden of greening their economy in this context? And is it fair that poor countries desperate to improve the lives of their citizens should be denied the elementary forms of energy that have sustained lifestyles in rich countries since the nineteenth century? The fundamental asymmetry between rich and poor countries is clear from just one piece of statistics cited in the latest (2021) report from the Intergovernmental Panel on Climate Change, which calculates that a 50 percent chance of keeping temperature rise below 2 degrees Celsius requires keeping total global emissions below 3.7 trillion tons; 2.4 trillion tons of this budget has already been emitted through industrialization and deforestation, mostly for the benefit of about a billion people in rich countries, so only 1.3 trillion tons out of the budget are left for more than six billion other people.

A great number of international technical and financial inducements will be necessary to encourage the decommissioning of coal plants in China and India or to stop deforestation in Brazil and Indonesia. At least the European Commission and the European Investment Bank have started talking about investing in green electrification programs in Africa, industrial decarbonization projects in Asia, and battery deployment in Latin America. It has been estimated that public and private investment in low-carbon projects in poor countries will need to be more than $1 trillion a year, more than six times the current rate of investment there. In order to induce private investors and cover risks, governments of rich countries promised several years back (but have so far not delivered) to provide grants and subsidies of about $100 billion—which is, of course, a formidable figure. But the consequences of not doing enough can be even more formidable for *both* rich and poor countries.

One positive development is that recently a group of banks, insurance firms, and asset management companies in forty-five countries, known as the Glasgow Financial Alliance for Net Zero and convened by the UN, has pledged large sums of capital toward net zero emission targets. Of course, they'll need some risk coverage from rich-country governments and international financial institutions, and any large private capital inflow in developing countries, even that for green causes, will need prudent regulations, both national and international. In addition to reduction of emissions, developing countries need money to adapt to rising sea levels and other extreme climate disasters. As First

Minister Nicola Sturgeon of Scotland reminded world leaders at the Twenty-Sixth UN Climate Change Conference in Glasgow in 2021, "Finance is key . . . not as an act of charity, but of reparation" for all the loss and damage caused by rich countries."

THE PATTERN AND DIRECTION
OF PUBLIC RESEARCH

In Chapter 7 we examined the relationship between social democracy and innovation, where public research is key. Possibly in partial reaction to the dramatic rise in Chinese investment in R&D, public spending on this is now rising in OECD countries after a long lag. The aim will be to spur innovations in artificial intelligence, synthetic biology, and clean energy (particularly in the generation and storage of decarbonized electricity, low-carbon methods of making cement and steel, and cheap scalable alternatives to powering planes and ships). Governments must take a proactive role in involving academic and private research institutions from different disciplines, announcing prizes for solving clearly defined problems and activating public research resources where the problems are not yet clearly defined, arranging for public equity shares in the commercialization of new ideas, and fomenting policy innovations beyond just pushing the technological frontier. In the diffusion of innovations through the economy, governments must play a major role in loosening existing intellectual property (IP) rights (e.g., by reducing the duration of patents or insisting on some disclosure requirements on key algorithms) when they block such diffusion and in providing adequate safety nets for disrupted livelihoods (as when new energy technology upends livelihoods in the existing fossil fuel, housing, and transportation sectors).

As I emphasized in Chapter 7, the *pattern* of innovations may be just as important as—if not more important than—the *rate* of innovations.

If in a social democracy workers have a strong voice in the running of a firm and also in the general polity outside it, it may be possible to re-direct investment in new technology from private firms and public authorities that better conform to social priorities—the creation of tech-nology that absorbs and empowers labor rather than replaces it, makes production more customized and labor-friendly, and pursues environ-mental, health, and other long-term goals instead of short-term profits, monopoly rights, and winner-take-all dynamics. For example, at present a handful of big tech companies account for more than two-thirds of the total global spending on artificial intelligence, which focuses largely on substituting algorithms for humans, setting the agenda for most research. Private investment in research does not take into ac-count the large social implications of the research outcome. As Daron Acemoglu and Pascual Restrepo (2020) have emphasized, excessive cor-porate concentration and the favorable tax treatment of capital also bias private research in socially unhelpful directions. A significant part of state-induced research, meanwhile, is in the use of artificial intelli-gence in surveillance technology that could undermine democratic freedoms. A social democratic state and labor institutions thus face a daunting but valuable task of redirecting research and the pattern of innovations.

Much of global R&D is spent in rich countries, and the technolog-ical results have spillover effects in the rest of the world. In developing countries, where the employment prospects of a large number of young workers have been hurt by the increasing capital intensity and skill in-tensity of technology generated in rich countries, public research and international financial assistance need to be oriented toward adaptation of the technology to use more local labor and resources. Additionally, artificial intelligence may be mobilized to improve and customize agri-cultural production methods to local crop, soil, and weather variations in poor countries or to allow teachers or nurses to perform more skilled, specialized tasks.

THE DECENTRALIZATION
OF GOVERNANCE

As I noted in Chapter 2, decentralization of governance is one way through which local people can "take back control." There has been a great deal of discussion in the past three decades on decentralized governance. Even apart from the widely debated issues of subsidiarity and devolution in the EU and states' rights in the United States, it has been at the center stage of policy experiments in many developing countries. Much of the empirical literature, particularly the local level evidence on the latter set of developing countries, has been reviewed by myself and Dilip Mookherjee (2015) and by Ghazala Mansuri and Vijayendra Rao (2013). To give one example, Brazil had introduced a participatory budgetary process (with citizens' direct input in budgeting and investment priorities) in a substantial fraction of municipalities. Sónia Gonçalves (2014) shows from a panel data set from all Brazilian municipalities over the years 1990–2004 that municipalities adopting such a budgetary process increased spending on health and sanitation significantly more than those that did not, and this already had sizable effects on outcomes like infant mortality. Many agree that this is an innovative and potentially empowering process that could be replicated elsewhere. It is not, however, easy to undertake. New York sought to establish its own participatory budgeting program, but its achievements were limited by lack of voter participation and knowledge. Technology can help here, as the example of the city of Reykjavik in Iceland shows: an online platform allows residents to suggest how money should be spent, and the majority of them participate. At its best, this kind of local program also has feedback effects on the nature of democracy itself; citizens participate more in civic affairs when they see more of a stake from doing so. Estonia and Taiwan are often cited as good examples of "digital democracy."

But, as the decentralization literature makes abundantly clear, much depends on the structures of power at the local level and the opportunities for democratic participation among common people. Even in rich countries, as noted in Chapter 2, there is often too much insider control in local bodies for zonal restrictions or professional licensing and "not in my backyard" resistance to new projects. There are many cases, in rich and poor countries alike, where it is easier for the elite or the oligarchs to capture the local than the federal government and where corruption and malfeasance can proliferate. As the underlying socioeconomic conditions vary from one area to another, chances of elite capture of local governments vary accordingly. One may think of possible institutional safeguards in the form of various accountability mechanisms, such as contested local elections; transparency of budgeting procedures; public provision of information; and oversight by citizen councils, judicial authorities, auditors, or media.

Local governments in poor countries are also afflicted by problems of local administrative capacity and adequate finance. Many federal or provincial governments are unwilling to devolve powers and funds to local governments, and so there is a big gap between de jure and de facto decentralization. It is not uncommon for higher-level governments to devolve responsibilities for social services to the lower level, without a corresponding devolution of funds or personnel—the notorious but frequent case of "unfunded mandates." Given the low taxable capacity at the local level in many poor countries, substantial financial devolution from above is thus imperative. In financial devolution it is often recommended that unconditional grants to local governments with random ex post audits may be the way to go to ensure enough local autonomy and flexibility.

One reason for low taxable capacity at the local level in developing countries is that the current system of taxation of local property is highly deficient. (In Latin America, for example, local property taxes collect only around 0.5 percent of GDP, whereas in Europe it is about 3 percent. In India the percentage is even lower, more like 0.15 percent.) The problems include poor or obsolete records, ambiguity about ownership, vast numbers of exemptions and concessions, and corruption in local tax administration, as a result of which tax collections are paltry. It is important to restructure and reform the whole system, with clear tax powers vested in local bodies. Reforms would include the computerization and updating of records, the use of geographic information systems to identify missing properties from the tax registry, the adoption of presumptive area-based valuation and periodic reassessment on some preannounced indexation rule (though taking care that the valuation is usually below market in view of unrealized capital gains), and giving priority to transparency and simplicity to make reforms seem fair and acceptable to the general public.

FIGHTING CORRUPTION TO BUILD
TRUST IN GOVERNANCE

In developing countries, particularly, the loss of public trust in democracy is associated with rampant corruption and widespread cynicism about the possibility of doing anything about it. Examples are far too many from places as diverse as Brazil, India, Mexico, Nigeria, and South Africa. The usual populist tropes about the "deep state" controlled by a corrupt official elite and the need to "take back control" are related to this.

Analysts have distinguished between *grand corruption* and *petty corruption*. *Grand corruption* involves large-scale political deals in which substantial money is exchanged between politicians (and their official accomplices) and those who seek their favor, often in the business world (including organized crime in some countries). *Petty corruption* refers to smaller-scale malfeasance mostly involving petty bureaucrats, inspectors, or policemen.

In the case of grand corruption, the cleaning up systems of election funding for politicians will be a major step, as I indicated at the end of

Chapter 7. It will be similarly difficult and important to reform procedures of bidding, auctions, and auditing in cases of large government procurement deals or purchases (e.g., in the case of military aircrafts or hardware) and the allocation of public resources that are highly valued (e.g., land or mineral resources or segments of the telecommunications spectrum). There is evidence, for example, in Ferraz and Finan (2008), that making audit reports on the use of federal funds in municipal governments publicly available in Brazil before elections reduces politicians' corruption.

Several countries have anticorruption investigative agencies, but more often than not they are not-quite independent of powerful political leaders. Independent investigative agencies with enough clout to follow through are, therefore, crucial; if they can unearth and publicize egregious cases involving the corrupt who are well connected, the automatic and cynical presumptions of people that nothing can be done in a democracy can be undermined. Some countries, however, have recently taken measures that move in the wrong direction, which does not bode well. India has seen the marginalization of the office of ombudsman (Lokpal) and the Information Commission—and worse, the partisan use of government investigative agencies to harass political opponents and dissenters. Brazil has seen the dissolution of Operação Lava Jato (Operation Car Wash)—the largest criminal investigation of corruption in the country's history—which lately came under a big political cloud. And in Indonesia the once formidable Corruption Eradication Commission has been defanged and lost credibility.

In the case of petty corruption that common people face on a day-to-day basis, digital technology may be a source of hope. In providing alternative sources of public service and ways of recording data, and in the general monitoring of transactions or operations, new technologies have been a great help in reducing the discretionary or arbitrary monopoly power of petty officials, which is a major source of their corruption. Here, too, there is a difference between corruption that takes the form of "speed money" (you bribe someone to push your file faster) and "collusive corruption" (you bribe someone to do something that they are not supposed to do). The latter—the more insidious variety— occurs, for example, when taxes are evaded, property value is under-assessed, and goods are smuggled or overinvoiced. In these cases the official connives at the problem or looks the other way. Such cases involve collusion between the bribe giver and the bribe taker to evade laws, and both parties gain. Neither is thus likely to report this to investigators, and it is hence much more difficult to root out. There are, however, some ways to minimize their toll. For example, in order to reduce the assessor's discretion in the matter of property value under-assessment, many municipal governments now use presumptive area-based valuation. In tax reform, separate and independent appellate bodies have been installed in some countries (e.g., Mexico). The assignment of multiple officials with overlapping jurisdictions to oversee a problem may also help; it has been reported that in the United States the overlapping involvement of local, state, and federal agencies in controlling illegal drugs has reduced police corruption.

International regulations also help. For example, the Foreign Corrupt Practices Act of 1977 in the United States has been a major deterrent to the bribing of officials in many countries by US-based international companies. In the German criminal law there are similar provisions for penalizing the bribing of foreign officials. Since large-scale corruption often has international ramifications that are inadequately handled by national courts, there is a proposal for an International Anti-Corruption Court that will investigate and prosecute corrupt officials when domestic governments are unwilling or unable to do so. Even with limited powers such a court could act as a partial deterrent to kleptocrats, the complicit multinational corporations, and the whole array of accountants, lawyers, and banks that bolster them. There should also be harmonization of attempts to regulate international money laundering through the buying up of high-end real estate in the cities of rich countries, enabled by anonymous shell corporations; these cities have long been the playground of an international klepto-cratic elite conniving with big banks and politicians.

THE NEED FOR INTERNATIONAL COORDINATION

As with corruption, we need a great deal of international coordination in environmental and health matters, as both have become increasingly urgent. In fighting the COVID-19 pandemic there have been some ex-emplary cases of international collaboration among medical researchers, health authorities, and pharmaceutical companies in sharing knowl-edge, methods of disease treatment, and vaccine development. Yet we have also seen cases of vaccine nationalism, and unseemly scrambles to corner scarce supplies of vaccine, mostly by rich countries—with stockpiles sometimes amounting to a few times the total size of their adult population (even when taking into account the need for booster shots). Poor countries, meanwhile, have been struggling to get any supplies at all. All of this is, of course, myopic even from the point of view of self-absorbed rich nations, as the vaccinated nations are not quite safe (particularly with the mounting probability of new variants of the virus emerging) as long as billions of people remain unvaccinated in the world. The rich countries' excess orders need to be immediately released and purchased for developing countries through some inter-national funding program.

In October 2020 India and South Africa approached the WTO to tem-porarily suspend parts of the Agreement on Trade-Related Aspects of Intellectual Property Rights (TRIPS) so that without the restrictive pat-ents enjoyed by the drug companies a much larger-scale global effort at manufacturing and distribution of vaccines could be carried out (even while paying royalties to the IP holders). This kind of waiver had helped the containment of the HIV / AIDS epidemic a couple of decades ago. The idea of a waiver was initially opposed by the EU, the United Kingdom, and the United States, though of late some politicians in those countries have turned favorable to the idea in the teeth of opposition by drug companies there. Even though the vaccine development process was mainly funded by the German, US, and other governments, the drug companies control most of the IP rights. The most egregious case is that of the firm Moderna, which was largely helped by public funds and government scientists in the United States in the development of the vaccine and yet has so far been quite obstructive in the implementation of the US government's announced policy of supplying vaccines to poor countries.

Apart from being restricted by patents, vaccine producers are also hampered by the reluctance of drug firms to share cell lines, data, and tacit know-how useful in production, as well as by export controls on ingredients. Vaccine manufacturing under *compulsory licensing,* which the WTO permits in public health emergencies, is often practically impossible in developing countries because of the large number of ingredients with separate IP protection in different countries (mRNA vaccines, for example, have more than a hundred components worldwide), even ignoring the real threats of sanctions countries face sometimes with such licensing.

In some ways more important than patent waivers is the issue of advance purchase commitment for developing countries (apart from their formidable problems of logistics in distribution). Drug companies with existing patents are not fully utilizing their production capacity for lack of preorders from poor countries, which need help in financing purchase commitments. The World Health Organization–backed COVID-19 Vaccine Global Access facility, funded (inadequately) through donations, to ensure fair global access to vaccines, had planned to distribute two billion doses (covering less than one-fifth of the target population) by the end of 2021, but struggled to distribute even only a quarter of that planned amount. At the current pace, widespread COVID-19 vaccination in developing countries is still on the distant horizon, not even accounting for the likelihood of new variants of the virus and the need for new vaccines in the near future.

It is also clear that in international coordination the role of many civil society organizations all around the globe is as important as that of governments. A good example is Gavi, the Vaccine Alliance, founded by the Gates Foundation, now an active network of governments, international organizations, businesses and nongovernmental organizations (NGOs). Since 2000 it has helped immunize more than eight hundred million children in developing countries against common childhood diseases.

In Chapter 3 we examined the need for multilateral rules on trade and capital flows. The WTO, which was hurt badly by the last American administration and by the trade wars and rampant protectionism of recent years, needs to be revived. Multilateral trade negotiation, for all the dominance by the corporate lobbies of rich countries, is better for poor countries than are bilateral deals, as poor countries' bargaining power in bilateral deals may be even lower. The restoration of broken trust among trading nations is a priority, and so is the need to restart the WTO Appellate Body for dispute settlement, which the United States has continued blocking. Additionally, flexibility in reforming old rules will be required to adapt to the changing needs of digital trade, e-commerce, and strategic investment in green energy and to the increased demand for resilience against supply-chain disruption; also needed will be general support for enabling micro-, small- and medium-size enterprises to benefit from trade.

Existing features like the Investor-State Dispute Settlement, which lobbyists of multinational corporations insert in international trade agreements to allow them to avoid national jurisdictions and thus skirt domestic rules and regulations, are clearly inconsistent with domestic labor interests in many countries. In general, the TRIPS regime needs to be seriously reformed and made less stringent for the purpose of helping innovations in new products both in rich and poor countries. As a large volume of academic research has shown, patents and the legal thickets around them hinder new innovations even in rich countries; one of the most forceful sets of counterarguments to patents has been made by Michele Boldrin and David Levine (2013).

To cope with the massive debt incurred by poor countries as a result of the pandemic, rich countries have to orchestrate a comprehensive and flexible debt restructuring. As the World Development Report 2022 indicates, developing countries face a looming crisis of a lost decade if international action in this matter turns out to be inadequate. The International Monetary Fund (IMF) has started issuing (up to a limit of $650 billion) its Special Drawing Rights, its global reserve asset. As a major part of this is allocated in proportion to IMF quotas, going mostly to high-income countries, the latter have to relend them to poor countries at highly concessional rates in order to assist them in their long and arduous road to recovery. One idea is for the rich countries to relend them through the IMF to the regional development banks, which have more experience with the local developing countries. So far the pace of progress in this has been very slow. One other area where the IMF needs to provide leadership in international coordination is in the sphere of digital currency: as it gains in importance in the near future, IMF guidance will be needed in defining the parameters of operation in foreign transactions and holdings in such currencies.

There is now increasing awareness that international coordination is also needed to govern the global supply chains that fragment the international production process, as these create more opportunities for regulatory arbitrage, more exploitative labor and environmental practices, and violation of human rights. There are now the (nonbinding) UN Guiding Principles on Business and Human Rights, which have been somewhat influential. The US Trade Facilitation and Trade Enforcement Act of 2015 has also been quite effective in making global companies accountable for human rights violations committed by dispersed legal entities in different jurisdictions. Similarly, there should be coordinated action (and international treaties with credible deterrents) among governments, public utilities, and businesses against cyberattacks, which have already become a serious danger for critical infrastructure.

In Chapter 3 we examined some issues of international coordination on immigration. There are some schemes afloat on limiting the flows of immigration to selected areas of specific skill shortages in rich countries and to some special humanitarian cases. For example, it has been proposed that rich countries will identify particular skill shortages at home—for example, certain kinds of nursing or caregiving service—and start funding training centers for such service workers located in poor countries. Then only a controlled number of them will be part of an immigration permit system, whereas the other such trained workers at those centers will serve the needs of their home countries. This will simultaneously relieve specific skill shortages in rich countries (at a lower cost than training workers at home) and help mitigate the impact of skill drain from poor countries. There are now some pilot programs started by the World Bank in developing countries to facilitate such controlled flows of migration. For example, there is one in Morocco that aims to strengthen the institutional capacity of its public employment agency to enable better preparation and placement of youth both in Morocco and in Germany.

International efforts at tax harmonization and coordination on financial regulations, and some restrictions on short-term capital flows, will have to be energetically pursued on a multilateral basis. In Chapter 7 I referred to issues of tax coordination, particularly on tax evasion by the rich and footloose global companies. There is now a concerted move to curb the age-old practice of *profit shifting* by global companies, which moves profits to subsidiaries in low-tax territories, and to make digital firms liable to taxation in places where their customers (and employees) are rather than where their headquarters are declared to be.

The *Economist* magazine reported (in its May 15, 2021, issue) that between 2000 and 2018, the share of foreign profits of American multinational firms booked in tax havens has doubled to 63 percent—that they now booked more profits in Bermuda than in China. The OECD has estimated, as stated in a 2018 report, that governments around the world are deprived of up to $240 billion every year by such rerouting of profits.

Contrary to the general impression that tax havens are usually exotic islands with palm trees, a large amount of corporate tax evasion and money laundering take place within rich countries; in the United States, the states of Delaware (and, later, South Dakota and Wyoming) have enabled some of the world's largest tax havens, as described in detail by Casey Michel in his 2021 book, *American Kleptocracy: How the US Created the World's Greatest Money Laundering Scheme in History*.

The OECD has started clamping down on some practices and loopholes. On the basis of an OECD proposal—see OECD (2021a)—for a global minimum tax on multinational corporations, both digital and nondigital, there has been a recent agreement among about 140 countries on a minimum tax of at least 15 percent on the largest firms. An improvement on the tax basis has also been suggested, to make corporations pay taxes based on the location of their sales, wherever their headquarters may be. Under this agreement the largest multinational companies with profit margins of at least 10 percent would have to allocate 20 percent of their global "superprofits" to countries where they sell their products and services; this sounds like a somewhat vague and (as regards revenue) restricted goal. Much, of course, will depend on the details (particularly relating to coverage of companies, tax thresholds and exemptions, a comprehensive definition of profits, etc.) of how these agreements are implemented (and the inevitable loopholes allowed for tax accountants to find), even if they survive the intense lobbying by the big firms and the low-tax countries. Appropriately designed, the minimum corporate tax may reduce harmful tax competition between countries, and tax avoidance by the corporations, but the benefit for most developing countries is rather low unless the minimum rate of taxation is raised and a bigger reallocation of global profits than what is proposed in the international agreement is arranged.

There is also need for some international coordination on competition policy. At the moment, in the matter of taxation of digital companies there is a scramble to get a share of their rent, putting the interests of different countries in conflict—see, for example, the disputes on this issue between the EU and the United States. Developing countries with little market power or collective bargaining strength lose out in the process. International multilateral agreements can try to ensure a reduction in monopoly power of digital companies and a more equitable distribution of the rent. Currently in some bilateral trade agreements the giant tech companies have succeeded in unobtrusively inserting data regulatory agenda biased in their favor. On the labor side, there is scope for international coordination on ensuring the observance of some International Labor Organization conventions on minimum labor standards, including discouraging (even penalizing) companies that interfere (all too often) with efforts to organize labor and bargain collectively.

On the global environmental front, progress has been slow on the curbing of greenhouse gas emissions. Thus far, there has been more talk, grandstanding, "greenwashing" (many of the green-labeled assets are not green at all) and rhetorical announcements of long-term goals like net zero emissions by 2050 than real and hard international time plan or trajectory of action (including research and capital investment). Such a plan has to be fair across countries and at the same time has to avoid "free rider" problems. Economists have made some proposals to resolve this, suggesting that countries emitting per capita more than the global average (usually the richer ones) should contribute to a global fund, while the below-average emitters (usually the poorer countries) will be paid out of that fund. This way some international fairness is achieved, and all countries, both rich and poor, will have an incentive to economize on emissions. Each country is then left free to follow its own emission restriction policy (carbon taxes, subsidies to renewables, or various domestic regulations) as their domestic politics permit. In the calculation of a country's per capita emissions (more relevant, per capita cumulative emissions since a recent cut-off date), those embodied in imports and exports should, of course, be properly taken into account. In general, to oversee the whole process we may need a new international institution dedicated to climate change issues, particularly in providing finance and helping in design and structuring of green projects and in coordinating the various green development banks that are coming up in different areas.

One also has to keep in mind that intergenerational justice in environmental matters is also intertwined with intragenerational justice issues. It has been estimated that the top decile of income earners in the world are responsible for nearly half of the total global carbon emissions. About half of the high-income polluters are in rich countries, and the other half mostly in middle-income countries. Thus, redistributive policies in these countries are also environmentally friendly.

On international action in the sphere of cultural malpractices, UN Secretary General António Guterres recently urged global action to build an alliance against the growth of neo-Nazis, white supremacists, and purveyors of hate speech and xenophobia everywhere. In Chapter 1 we examined the toxic role of social media in this respect. In some poor countries social media have been widely charged for fomenting inter-community violence and riots. Even in rich countries there is a brewing uproar against the role of big tech companies as facilitators in spreading hate and lies. Some regulations on internet governance are likely, particularly as the current ones on digital media are more lax than those on conventional media (the recent Digital Services Act of the European Union has shown a way). But, at least in the United States, nobody underestimates the big tech companies' lobbying power and their financial grip over influential members of the US Congress. Some people have more hope on pressure (and whistleblowing) from the rank and file of workers within some of these companies (as recent events among workers inside Facebook and Google seem to suggest).

Even if the big tech companies were to be somewhat tamed, there is a growing danger of authoritarian and semiauthoritarian countries taking this opportunity to put stringent control over the social media to censor out inconvenient information and circulate misinformation to their advantage. Authoritarian China has already shown the way in this. The big danger to democracy in the near future is from surveillance and control by the state, enabled with digital technology and artificial intelligence and weaponizing its troll army and cyber-robots. There is a great need for some international agreements on minimum regulations that can help us achieve the delicate balance between mitigating the spread of misinformation, on the one hand, and the censoring and repression of dissent and protest, on the other. It is very difficult to achieve a solution that will satisfy everybody, but an international agreement can define the contours of minimum safeguards and standards. There are some things to learn from the work of the coalition called the Global Network Initiative, which has tried for many years to set a code of conduct for tech and telecommunications companies to protect online speech and privacy globally.

THE ROLE OF LABOR ORGANIZATIONS FOR STEPPING INTO THE CULTURAL VOID

In Chapter 1 we examined the growing cultural gulf between professional and low-skill workers. We have to mobilize labor organizations to try to bridge this gulf instead of leaving them to serve only as narrow wage-bargaining platforms or lobbies. They may take an active role in local cultural life, involving the neighborhood community and religious organizations, as they used to do in some European and Latin American countries. As I noted in Chapters 2 and 6, this is one way unions enabled workers to tame and transcend their parochial nativist passions and prejudices against minorities and immigrants. The decline of unions in recent years has not only weakened workers' economic bargaining power but has also hollowed out the individual worker's sense of belonging to a shared institution that provided some meaning and identity in her life. All over the world, young people, in particular, are seeking community and shared purpose. In the absence of leadership, or alternative cultural visions or purposive programs (e.g., paid community service in civic programs of various kinds), they are straying into absolutist mission-led ventures like the so-called Alt-Right in Germany or the United States or becoming jihadist Muslims or Hindu militants in India. Labor movements have to play a constructive role in this cultural void. Leftists who talk only of policies but not of values are often ceding ground to their opposition.

A return to community norms and cultural visions, without encouraging exclusivity and barriers is, of course, a delicate task. Let's take, for example, the larger imagined political community of the nation. Workers may legitimately feel pride in their national autonomy and cultural history, but one has to be careful that such pride does not derive its oxygen from the majoritarian ethnicity, marginalizing minorities or demonizing foreign countries or cultures. In Chapter 3 we examined civic nationalism, which combines pride in one's cultural distinctiveness (and maybe soccer teams) without giving up on some shared universal humanitarian values (including tolerance for the diversity evident on those soccer teams).

One of those universal values may relate to some *procedural* aspects of liberal democracy—ensuring equal dignity for all human beings and their equal access to due process under the rule of law—as opposed to merely the *participatory*, or majoritarian, aspects. Enthusiasts for the latter often complain about the dominance of unelected elite experts or an insulated technocracy (and a suspected "deep state"). One clearly has to strike a balance between the need for evidence- and knowledge-based governance in many complex situations where expert advice may be indispensable and the need for frequent resort to exercises in popular accountability.

Shared values, of course, require some trust in shared information. In a world of virulent disinformation and fake news, with social media amplifying anger and resentments, labor organizations should also be active in lobbying for—and, if necessary, supplying—links to public information services and to news provided by demonstrably independent agencies that could, over time, earn the trust of the majority (or develop "herd immunity" against the "virus" of fake news). In the 2020 Taiwanese presidential and legislative elections, the way civil society organizations combatted massive Chinese divisive and disinformation campaigns—detecting, debunking, and blocking fake news online—is a positive recent example of how labor organizations in collaboration with NGOs can play a crucial role.

Labor and religious organizations could also find common cause around the delivery of social services and protecting the environment. In fact, religious and charitable organizations often try to make up for the lack (or deficiencies) of social services at the local level from government agencies run by unionized public-sector employees. Coordination may be more productive here. As I noted in Chapter 1, in Egypt, India, or Indonesia, Hindu or Muslim faith-based organizations became popular by providing much-needed basic educational and health services for the local poor, while unionized government workers in those sectors had become corrupt, inept, or truant. Public-sector unions are important, but they must prioritize their most vulnerable constituents, coordinate with other providers, and work to protect both their workers and their needy customers.

In addition, as I noted in Chapter 6, in carrying out policies like affirmative action for underprivileged groups more open attitudes about poor workers from the ethnic *majority* communities, along with more sensitivity to the new fissures, may assuage the resentment about liberals caring only for minorities and immigrants. Labor organizations can try to accommodate such policies that give priority to economic justice and relieve some identity-based tension by making all of this a part of a common goal of humanitarian uplift and citizenship rather than a sectarian agenda of catering to some particular social groups. This is very important in persuading some people, like Arlie Hochschild's (2016) respondents, referred to in Chapter 1, who keep complaining that Black people and Hispanics are "cutting lines," or the less successful members of dominant caste groups in India who are currently agitating for preferential treatment in public jobs on par with the historically marginalized castes. As I noted in Chapter 6, balancing the interests of the aggrieved sections of the majority and of chronically oppressed minorities is difficult, but doable, if approached with some finesse and openness to compromise.

There have also been conflicts between environmentalists and workers on the issue of jobs. But a reallocation of jobs (with appropriate subsidized retraining) toward renewable energy industries, which happen to be more labor intensive than the ones preserved by the current fossil fuel subsidies, is eminently possible. Working with local cultural and religious organizations, it may also be feasible to raise environmental awareness as part of the long-term interest of workers, since most of the current and future victims of environmental degradation on the local commons and global climate change are poor workers.

Labor organizations and related social movements could thus channel the economic anxiety of workers in civic directions, diverting them from the colorful ethnonationalist narratives that demagogues use to mobilize this anxiety. They could be sensitive to the genuine communitarian needs and the cultural neglect that workers feel in their relation with cosmopolitan liberal leaders.

All of this is, of course, easier said than done. The task before us is indeed daunting. We can proceed with the thought, paraphrasing what Antonio Gramsci wrote from Benito Mussolini's prison cell, that the challenge for us is not to have illusions, and yet not to be disillusioned.

In this chapter, I have touched upon only a small number policy issues arising from the pervasive economic and cultural insecurity. I have left out many other kinds of insecurity from our consideration. As I mentioned at the end of Chapter 1, there are multiple kinds of sheer physical insecurity—from ecological distress, wars and civil wars, terrorism and crime, to cyberattacks against critical infrastructure and the like—that are uppermost in many minds in different parts of the world. This is not to speak of the much bigger existential risks looming in the not-too-distant future for humanity: the possibility of nuclear destruction, climate collapse, engineered pandemics, and rogue or what is called unaligned (as in, unaligned with human values) artificial intelligence.

Faced with these massive uncertainties and insecurities it is easy to be overwhelmed. But the long story of human perseverance and resilience is also impressive.

In 1941, in the midst of the devastation and misery of the Second World War, and only a few months before his death, Rabindranath Tagore said in his last speech, "The Crisis in Civilization," (1941) "As I look around I see the crumbling ruins of a proud civilization strewn like a vast heap of futility. And yet I shall not commit the grievous sin of losing faith in Man."

References

Acemoglu, D., S. Johnson, and J. Robinson. 2005. "The Rise of Europe: Atlantic Trade, Institutional Change, and Economic Growth." *American Economic Review* 95 (3): 546–579.

Acemoglu, D., and P. Restrepo. 2020. "The Wrong Kind of AI? Artificial Intelligence and the Future of Labor Demand." *Cambridge Journal of Regions, Economy and Society* 13 (1): 25–35.

Aghion, P., J. Cai, M. Dewatripont, L. Du, A. Harrison, and P. Legros. 2015. "Industrial Policy and Competition." *American Economic Journal: Macroeconomics* 7 (4): 1–32.

Alesina, A., A. Miano, and S. Stantcheva. 2019. "Immigration and Redistribution." NBER Working Paper 24733, National Bureau of Economic Research, Cambridge, MA.

Algan, Y., S. Guriev, E. Papaioannou, and E. Passari. 2017. "The European Trust Crisis and the Rise of Populism." *Brookings Papers on Economic Activity* 48 (2): 309–400.

Allcott, H., and M. Gentzkow. 2017. "Social Media and Fake News." *Journal of Economic Perspectives* 31 (2): 211–236.

Altenburg, T., and C. Assmann, eds. 2017. *Green Industrial Policy: Concept, Policies, Country Experiences.* UN Environment Program, Geneva, and German Development Institute, Bonn.

Ambedkar, B. R. (1950) 2007. *Dr. Babasaheb Ambedkar Writings and Speeches*, ed. D. C. Ahir. Delhi: B.R. Publishing.

Arendt, H. (1973) 2013. *Hannah Arendt: The Last Interview and Other Conversations.* New York: Melville House.

Autor, D., D. Dorn, G. Hanson, and K. Majlesi. 2020. "Importing Political Polarization? The Electoral Consequences of Rising Trade Exposure." *American Economic Review* 110 (10): 3139–3183.

Bandiera, O., A. Prat, and T. Valletti. 2009. "Active and Passive Waste in Government Spending: Evidence from a Policy Experiment." *American Economic Review* 99 (4): 1278–1308.

Bandyopadhyay, S., and E. Green. 2016. "Pre-colonial Political Centralization and Contemporary Development in Uganda." *Economic Development and Cultural Change* 64 (3): 471–508.

Bardhan, P. 1984. *The Political Economy of Development in India.* Oxford: Basil Blackwell.

Bardhan, P. 2013. *Awakening Giants, Feet of Clay: Assessing the Economic Rise of China and India.* Princeton, NJ: Princeton University Press.

Bardhan, P., and D. Mookherjee. 2015. "Decentralization and Development: Dilemmas, Trade-offs, and Safeguards." In *Handbook of Multilevel Finance,* ed. E. Ahmad and G. Brosio: 461–470. Northampton, MA: Edward Elgar.

Bardhan, P., and D. Mookherjee. 2020. "Clientelistic Politics and Economic Development: An Overview." In *The Handbook of Economic Development and Institutions,* ed. J-M Baland, F. Bourguignon, J-P. Platteau, and T. Verdier: 84–102. Princeton, NJ: Princeton University Press.

Bates, R. H. 2008. *When Things Fell Apart: State Failure in Late-Century Africa.* New York: Cambridge University Press.

Bell, D. A. 2016. *The China Model: Political Meritocracy and the Limits of Democracy.* Princeton, NJ: Princeton University Press.

Besley, T., and T. Persson. 2011. *Pillars of Prosperity: The Political Economics of Development Clusters.* Princeton, NJ: Princeton University Press.

Bloomberg. "Bloomberg Billionaires Index." n.d. https://www.bloomberg.com/billionaires/

Bockstette, V., A. Chanda, and L. Putterman. 2002. "States and Markets: The Advantage of an Early Start." *Journal of Economic Growth* 7 (4): 347–369.

Boldrin, M., and D. K. Levine. 2013. "The Case against Patents." *Journal of Economic Perspectives* 27 (1): 3–22.

Brass, P. R. 2003. *The Production of Hindu-Muslim Violence in Contemporary India.* Seattle: University of Washington Press.

Brenan, M. 2021. "Approval of Labor Unions at Highest Point since 1965." September 2, 2021. https://news.gallup.com/poll/354455/approval-labor-unions-highest-point-1965.aspx

Cagé, J. 2020. *The Price of Democracy: How Money Shapes Politics and What to Do about It.* Cambridge, MA: Harvard University Press.

Cao, Y. 2021. "The Social Costs of Patronage Ties: Lessons from the Sichuan Earthquake." Working paper, Boston University, November 2021.

Card, D., J. Kluve, and A. Weber. 2010. "Active Labor Market Policy Evaluations: A Meta-Analysis." *Economic Journal* 120: F452–477.

Cato Institute. "Human Freedom Index 2021." https://www.cato.org/human -freedom-index/2021

Chen, T., and J. K. Kung. 2018. "Busting the 'Princelings': The Campaign against Corruption in China's Primary Land Market." *Quarterly Journal of Economics* 134 (1): 185–226.

Chetty, R., D. Grusky, M. Hell, N. Hendren, R. Manduca, and J. Naran. 2017. "The Fading American Dream: Trends in Absolute Income Mobility since 1940." *Science* 356 (6336): 398–406.

Coka, D. A., and T. Rausch. 2020. *Gains, Pains and Divides: Attitudes on Globalization on the Eve of the Corona Crisis.* 2020 GED Globalization Survey. https://www .bertelsmann-stiftung.de/fileadmin/files/user_upload/MT_Globalization _Survey_2020_ENG.pdf

Colantone, I., and P. Stanig. 2018. "The Trade Origins of Economic Nationalism: Import Competition and Voting Behavior in Western Europe." *American Journal of Political Science* 62 (4): 936–953.

Companiesmarketcap.com. n.d. "Largest Tech Companies by Market Cap." https://companiesmarketcap.com/tech/largest-tech-companies-by-market -cap/

Connaughton, A., N. Kent, and S. Schumacher. 2020. "How People around the World See Democracy in 8 Charts." Pew Research Center. February 27, 2020. https://www.pewresearch.org/fact-tank/2020/02/27/how-people -around-the-world-see-democracy-in-8-charts/

Cornell University, INSEAD, and WIPO. 2019. "Global Innovation Index 2019: Creating Healthy Lives—The Future of Medical Innovation." World Intellectual Property Organization. https://www.wipo.int/publications/en /details.jsp?id=4434

Cornick, J. 2013. "Public Sector Capabilities and Organization for Successful PDP's." Washington, DC: Inter-American Development Bank.

Covarrubias, M., G. Gutiérrez, and T. Philippon. 2019. "From Good to Bad Concentration? U.S. Industries over the Past 30 Years." NBER Working Paper 25983, National Bureau of Economic Research, Cambridge, MA.

Crawford, J., L. Menand, and M. Ricks. 2021. "FedAccounts: Digital Dollars." *George Washington Law Review* 89 (1): 113–172.

Cullenward, D., and D. G. Victor. 2020. *Making Climate Policy Work.* New York: Polity Books.

Damgaard, J., T. Elkjaer, and N. Johannesen. 2019. "What Is Real and What Is Not in the Global FDI Network." Working Paper no. 19/274, International Monetary Fund, Washington D.C.

Defoe, D. 1722. *A Journal of the Plague Year.* London. https://www.gutenberg.org/files/376/376-h/376-h.htm

Devlin, K., and C. Johnson. 2019. "Indian Elections Nearing amid Frustrations with Politics, Concerns about Misinformation." Pew Research Center. March 25, 2019. https://www.pewresearch.org/fact-tank/2019/03/25/indian-elections-nearing-amid-frustration-with-politics-concerns-about-misinformation/

Dincecco, M., and G. Katz. 2016. "State Capacity and Long-Run Economic Performance." *Economic Journal* 126 (590): 189–218.

Dijkstra, L., H. Poelman, and A. Rodríguez-Pose. 2020. "The Geography of EU Discontent." *Regional Studies* 54 (6): 737–753.

Di Tella, R., J. Dubra, and A. Lagomarsino. 2019. "Meet the Oligarchs: Business Legitimacy, State Capacity, and Taxation." Working paper, Harvard University.

Economist, 2016. "What the World Thinks about Globalization." November 18, 2016. https://www.economist.com/graphic-detail/2016/11/18/what-the-world-thinks-about-globalisation

Ehrenreich, B. 1989. *Fear of Falling: The Inner Life of the Middle Class.* New York: Pantheon Books.

Engineer, A. A., ed. 1984. *Communal Riots in Post-Independence India.* Hyderabad: Sangam Books.

Evans, P., and J. Rauch. 1999. "Bureaucracy and Growth: A Cross-National Analysis of the Effects of 'Weberian' State Structures on Economic Growth." *American Sociological Review* 64: 748–765.

Ferraz, C., and F. Finan. 2008. "Exposing Corrupt Politicians: The Effect of Brazil's Publicly Released Audits on Electoral Outcomes." *Quarterly Journal of Economics* 123 (2): 703–745.

Fisman, R., and Y. Wang. 2015. "The Mortality Costs of Political Connections." *Review of Economic Studies,* no. 82: 1346–1382.

Foa, R. S., A. Klassen, M. Slade, A. Rand, R. and Collins. 2020. *Global Satisfaction with Democracy Report 2020.* Cambridge: Centre for the Future of Democracy. https://www.cam.ac.uk/system/files/report2020_003.pdf

Friedman, M. 1962. *Capitalism and Freedom.* Chicago: University of Chicago Press.

Friedman, M. 1994. "Introduction." In *Road to Serfdom,* ed. F. A. Hayek: ix–xx. Chicago: University of Chicago Press.

Fujiwara, T., and L. Wantchekon. 2013. "Can Informed Public Deliberation Overcome Clientelism? Experimental Evidence from Benin." *American Economic Journal: Applied Economics* 5 (4): 241–255.

Gandhi, M. K. 1909. *Hind Swaraj or Indian Home Rule.* Ahmedabad: Navajivan Publishing House.

Galiani, S., P. Gertler, and E. Schargrodsky. 2008. "School Decentralization: Helping the Good Get Better but Leaving the Poor Behind." *Journal of Public Economics* 92 (10–11): 2106–2120.

Gallup. 2020. *Back to Work: Listening to Americans.* https://www.gallup.com /analytics/329573/back-to-work-listening-to-americans.aspx

Gonçalves, S. 2014. "The Effects of Participatory Budgeting on Municipal Expenditures and Infant Mortality in Brazil." *World Development* 63 (1): 94–110.

Gramsci, A. 2011. *Prison Notebooks* (full translation). New York: Columbia University

Guha, R. 2000. *The Unquiet Woods: Ecological Change and Peasant Resistance in the Himalaya.* Berkeley: University of California Press.

Halpin, J. "Immigration Is Contentious across the World." *The Liberal Patriot.* December 16, 2021. YouGov Global Progress 2021 Survey on Immigration: https://theliberalpatriot.substack.com/p/immigration-is-contentious -across?utm_source=url

Haney López, I. 2019. *Merge Left: Fusing Race and Class, Winning Elections, and Saving America.* New York: New Press.

Harding, R., and D. Stasavage. 2014. "What Democracy Does (and Doesn't Do) for Basic Services: School Fees, School Inputs, and African Elections." *Journal of Politics* 76 (1): 229–245.

Harrison, A., and A. Rodríguez-Clare. 2010. "Trade, Foreign Investment, and Industrial Policy for Developing Countries." In *Handbook of Development Economics,* vol. 5, ed. D. Rodrik and M. Rosenzweig: 4039–4214. Amsterdam: Elsevier.

Hayek, F. A. 1960. *Why I Am Not a Conservative.* Chicago: University of Chicago Press.

Heritage Foundation. 2022. Economic Freedom Index. "Country Rankings." https://www.heritage.org/index/ranking

Hirschman, A. O. 1977. *The Passions and the Interests: Political Arguments for Capitalism before its Triumph.* Princeton, NJ: Princeton University Press.

Hobsbawm, E., and T. Ranger, ed. 2012. *The Invention of Tradition.* Cambridge: Cambridge University Press.

Hochschild, A. R. 2016. *Strangers in Their Own Land: Anger and Mourning on the American Right.* New York: New Press

Houellebecq, M. 2015. *Submission.* New York: Farrar, Straus & Giroux.

Hurun. 2020. "China Rich List 2020." Hurun Research Institute, Shanghai. 2020
    https://hurun.net/en-US/Info/Detail?num=1E096ECED920
Hurun. 2020. "India Rich List." Hurun Research Institute, Mumbai. 2020.
    https://www.hurun.net/en-US/Info/Detail?num=514894A6274C
ILO (International Labour Organization). 2021. "Social Protection Spotlight."
    January 2021. https://www.social-protection.org/gimi/RessourcePDF
    .action?id=57143
ILO (International Labour Organization). n.d. "Youth Labour Statistics."
    https://ilostat.ilo.org/topics/youth/
Im, Z. J., N. Mayer, B. Palier, and J. Rovny. 2019. "The 'Losers of Automation':
    A Reservoir of Votes for the Radical Right?" *Research and Politics* 6 (1): 1–7.
India. National Statistical Office. 2021. "Periodic Labor Force Survey—Annual
    Report [July 2019–June 2020." https://pib.gov.in/PressReleaseIframePage
    .aspx?PRID=1738163
Inter-Governmental Panel on Climate Change, Sixth Assessment Report. 2021.
International Monetary Fund. 2017. *Fiscal Monitor: Tackling Inequality.* October 2017.
    https://www.imf.org/en/Publications/FM/Issues/2017/10/05/fiscal
    -monitor-october-2017
Jäger, S., B. Schoefer, and J. Heining. 2021. "Labor in the Boardroom." *Quarterly
    Journal of Economics* 136 (2): 669–725.
Jenner, W. J. F. 1992. *The Tyranny of History: The Roots of China's Crisis.* London:
    Penguin Books.
Jia, R., and H. Nie. 2015. "Decentralization, Collusion, and Coalmine." *Review of
    Economics and Statistics* 99 (1): 105–118.
Kapur, D. 2020. "Why Does the Indian State Both Fail and Succeed?" *Journal of
    Economic Perspectives* 34 (1): 31–54.
Keynes, J. M. 1936. *The General Theory of Employment, Interest, and Money.*
    London: Palgrave Macmillan.
Khosla, M. 2020. *India's Founding Moment: The Constitution of a Most Surprising
    Democracy.* Cambridge, MA: Harvard University Press.
Krugman, P. 2016. "What Happened on Election Day." *New York Times,* November 8,
    2016.
Kruse, D. L., R. B. Freeman, and J. R. Blasi., eds. 2010. *Shared Capitalism at Work:
    Employee Ownership, Profit and Gain Sharing, and Broad-based Stock Options.*
    Chicago: University of Chicago Press.
Landry, P. F., X. Lu, and H. Duan. 2017. "Does Performance Matter? Evaluating
    Political Selection along the Chinese Administrative Ladder." *Comparative
    Political Studies* 51 (8): 1074–1105.

Larsen, C. A. 2017. "Revitalizing the 'Civic' and 'Ethnic' Distinction: Perceptions of Nationhood across Two Dimensions, 44 Countries and Two Decades." *Nations and Nationalism* 23 (4): 970–993.

Levi, M. 1988. *Of Rule and Revenue*. Berkeley: University of California Press.

Levitsky, S., and D. Ziblatt. 2018. *How Democracies Die*. New York: Crown.

Li, J. S. 2003. "Relation-Based versus Rule-Based Governance: An Explanation of East Asian Miracle and Asian Crisis." *Review of International Economics* 11 (4): 651–673.

Lilla, M. 2018. *The Once and Future Liberal: After Identity Politics*. New York: Harper Collins.

Mahler, D. G., N. Yonzan, C. Lakner, R. A. Castaneda Aguilar, and H. Wu. 2021. "Updated Estimates of the Impact of COVID-19 on Global Poverty." World Bank Blogs. June 24, 2021. https://blogs.worldbank.org/opendata/updated-estimates-impact-covid-19-global-poverty-turning-corner-pandemic-2021

Mann, T. 1938. *The Coming Victory of Democracy*. New York: Knopf

Mansuri, G., and V. Rao. 2013. *Localizing Development: Does Participation Work?* Washington, DC: World Bank.

Margalit, Y. 2019. "Economic Insecurity and the Causes of Populism, Reconsidered." *Journal of Economic Perspectives* 33 (4): 152–170.

Martinez-Bravo, M., G. Padró i Miquel, N. Qian, and Y. Yao. 2014. "Political Reform in China: Elections, Public Goods and Income Distribution." Unpublished manuscript, March 3, 2014. https://economics.harvard.edu/files/economics/files/qian-nancy_3-5-14_political_reform_in_china_elections_public_good_and_income_distribution_3-3-2014.pdf

Marx, K. (1867) 1977. *Capital: A Critique of Political Economy*, Vol. I. New York: Vintage Books.

Mazzucato, M. 2015. *The Entrepreneurial State: Debunking Public Vs. Private Sector Myths*. New York: Public Affairs.

McKinsey Global Institute. *Report on The Future of Work after COVID-19*. February 18, 2021. https://www.mckinsey.com/featured-insights/future-of-work/the-future-of-work-after-covid-19

Michalopoulos, S., and E. Papaioannou. 2013. "Pre-colonial Ethnic Institutions and Contemporary African Development." *Econometrica* 81 (1): 113–152.

Michel, C. 2021. *American Kleptocracy: How the US Created the World's Greatest Money Laundering Scheme in History*. New York: St. Martin's Press.

Milanović, B. 2019. *Capitalism Alone: The Future of the System That Rules the World*. Cambridge, MA: Harvard University Press.

Mishra, P. 2017. *Age of Anger: A History of the Present*. New York: Farrar, Straus & Giroux.

Moore, B. 1966. *Social Origins of Dictatorship and Democracy: Lord and Peasant in the Making of the Modern World*. Boston: Beacon Press.

Mukand, S. W., and D. Rodrik. 2020. "The Political Economy of Liberal Democracy." *Economic Journal* 130 (2): 765–792.

Mundle, S., and S. Sikdar. 2019. "Subsidies, Merit Goods, and the Fiscal Space for Reviving Growth." *Economic Political Weekly* 55 (5): 52–60.

Muralidharan, K., P. Niehaus, and S. Sukhtankar. 2014. "Payments Infrastructure and the Performance of Public Programs: Evidence from Biometric Smartcards in India." NBER Working Paper 19999, National Bureau of Economic Research, Cambridge, MA.

National Center for Social Research. "British Social Attitudes 37." 2021. https://natcen.ac.uk/our-research/research/british-social-attitudes/

Ochsner, C., and F. Rosel. 2019. "Mobilizing History." Unpublished manuscript, University of Zurich.

OECD. 2016. *The Risk of Automation for Jobs in OECD Countries*. https://www.oecd-ilibrary.org/docserver/5jlz9h56dvq7-en.pdf?expires=1647395678&id=id&accname=guest&checksum=FBD4429425186BC2FE86A987DA4E25B5

OECD. 2018. "Market Concentration." Issues paper by the Secretariat. June 6–8, 2018. https://one.oecd.org/document/DAF/COMP/WD(2018)46/en / pdf

OECD. 2020. *International Community Continues Making Progress against Offshore Tax Evasion*. June 30, 2020. https://www.oecd.org/tax/transparency/documents/international-community-continues-making-progress-against-offshore-tax-evasion.htm

OECD. 2021a. *Inheritance Taxation in OECD Countries*. May 11, 2021. https://www.oecd.org/tax/tax-policy/inheritance-taxation-in-oecd-countries-e2879a7d-en.htm

OECD. 2021b. "International Collaboration to End Tax Avoidance." November 4, 2021. https://www.oecd.org/tax/beps/

Ortiz-Ospina, E., and M. Roser. 2016. "Trust." https://ourworldindata.org/trust

Osafo-Kwaako, P., and J. A. Robinson. 2013. "Political Centralization in Pre-colonial Africa." *Journal of Comparative Economics* 41 (1): 6–21.

"Pandemic Preparedness and COVID-19." 2022. *The Lancet*. February 1, 2022. https://www.thelancet.com/journals/lancet/article/PIIS0140-6736(22)00172-6/fulltext

Piketty, T. 2020. *Capital and Ideology*. Cambridge, MA: Belknap Press.

Rajan, R. 2019. *The Third Pillar: How Markets and the State Leave the Community Behind*. New York: Penguin Press.

Rajan, R., and L. Zingales. 2003. *Saving Capitalism from the Capitalists: Unleashing the Power of Financial Markets to Create Wealth and Spread Opportunity*. New York: Crown Business.

Rasul, I., and D. Rogger. 2018. "Management of Bureaucrats and Public Service Delivery: Evidence from the Nigerian Civil Service." *Economic Journal* 128 (608): 413–446.

Schneider, H., and C. Kahn. 2020. "Majority of Americans Favor Wealth Tax on Very Rich: Reuters / Ipsos Poll." January 10, 2020. https://www.reuters.com /article/us-usa-election-inequality-poll/majority-of-americans-favor-wealth -tax-on-very-rich-reuters-ipsos-poll-idUSKBN1Z9141

Sanyal, P., and V. Rao. 2018. *Oral Democracy: Deliberation in Indian Village Assemblies.* Cambridge: Cambridge University Press.

Scheuer, F., and J. Slemrod. 2021. "Taxing Our Wealth." *Journal of Economic Perspectives* 35 (1): 207–230.

Scheve, K., and D. Stasavage. 2016. *Taxing the Rich: A History of Fiscal Fairness in the United States and Europe.* Princeton, NJ: Princeton University Press.

Shum, D. 2021. *Red Roulette: An Insider's Story of Wealth, Power, Corruption and Vengeance in Today's China.* New York: Simon & Schuster.

Schumpeter, J. 1942. *Capitalism, Socialism and Democracy.* New York: Harper & Brothers.

Scott, J. C. 2014. *Two Cheers for Anarchism: Six Easy Pieces on Autonomy, Dignity, and Meaningful Work and Play.* Princeton, NJ: Princeton University Press.

Scruton, R. 2017. *On Human Nature.* Princeton, NJ: Princeton University Press.

Sen, A. 1999. *Development as Freedom.* Oxford: Oxford University Press.

Sokoloff, K. L., and S. L. Engerman. 2000. "Institutions, Factor Endowments, and Paths of Development in the New World." *Journal of Economic Perspectives* 14 (3): 217–232.

Stokes, B. 2017. " Public Divided on Prospects for Next Generation." Pew Research Center. June 5, 2017. https://www.pewresearch.org/global/2017 /06/05/2-public-divided-on-prospects-for-the-next-generation/

Su, F., and R. Tao. 2016. "Meritocracy and Patronage in State Building: Evidence from Provincial Leaders in China." Renmin University, Beijing, unpublished paper.

Subramanian, S. 2020. "Doing the Maths: Why India Should Introduce a Covid Wealth Tax on the Ultra-rich." *Scroll.in,* April 16, 2020. https://scroll.in /article/959314/doing-the-maths-why-india-should-introduce-a-covid -wealth-tax-on-the-ultra-rich

Tagore, R. (1916) 1917. *Nationalism.* London: Macmillan

Tagore, R. 1941. *Crisis in Civilization.* Calcutta: Visva-Bharati

Tamir, Y. 2019. "Not So Civic: Is There a Difference between Ethnic and Civic Nationalism?" *Annual Review of Political Science,* no. 22, 419–434.

Taylor, C. 1989. "Atomism." In C. Taylor, ed., *Philosophy and the Human Sciences: Philosophical Papers 2:* 187–210. Cambridge: Cambridge University Press.

Temin, P. 2017. *The Vanishing Middle Class: Prejudice and Power in a Dual Economy.* Cambridge, MA: MIT Press.

Thachil, T. 2016. *Elite Parties, Poor Voters: How Social Services Win Votes in India.* Cambridge: Cambridge University Press.

Tilly, C. 1985. "War Making and State Making as Organized Crime." In *Bringing the State Back In,* ed. P. Evans, D. Rueschemeyer, and T. Skocpol: 169–191 New York: Cambridge University Press.

UK Government Treasury Department. 2007. "Tax Advantaged Employee Share Schemes: Analysis of Productivity Effects." H. M. Revenue and Customs Research Paper.

US Bureau of Labor Statistics. 2020. "Labor Force Statistics from the Current Population Survey." https://www.bls.gov/cps/lfcharacteristics.htm

V-Dem Institute. 2021. *Autocratization Turns Viral: Democracy Report 2021.* Gothenburg, Sweden: University of Gothenburg.

Verniers, G., and C. Jaffrelot. 2020. "The Reconfiguration of Indian Political Elite: Profiling the 17th Lok Sabha." *Contemporary South Asia* 28 (2): 242–254.

Wade, R. 1990. *Governing the Market: Economic Theory and the Role of Government in East Asian Industrialization.* Princeton, NJ: Princeton University Press.

Wantchekon, L. 2003. "Clientelism and Voting Behavior: Evidence from a Field Experiment in Benin." *World Politics* 55 (3): 399–422.

Weber, E. 1976. *Peasants into Frenchmen: The Modernization of Rural France 1870–1914.* Stanford: Stanford University Press.

Wire. 2018. "Real or Fake, We Can Make Any Message Go Viral: Amit Shah to BJP Social Media Volunteers." *Wire,* September 26, 2018.

World Development Report 2022: Finance for an Equitable Recovery. 2022. Washington, DC: World Bank

World Economic Outlook Report, April 2017: Gaining Momentum? Washington, DC: International Monetary Fund.

World Inequality Report (published annually). Paris: Paris School of Economics

World Uncertainty Index (published every Quarter). London: Economist Intelligence Unit. https://worlduncertaintyindex.com/

Xu, C. 2011. "The Fundamental Institutions of China's Reforms and Development." *Journal of Economic Literature* 49 (4): 1076–1151.

YouGov Cambridge Globalism Project—Conspiracy Theories. 2019. https://d25d2506sfb94s.cloudfront.net/cumulus_uploads/document/2c6lta5kbu/YouGov%20Cambridge%20Globalism%20Project%20-%20Conspiracy%20Theories.pdf

Zuboff, S. 2020. "You are Now Remotely Controlled." *New York Times,* January 20, 2020.

Acknowledgments

Apart from expressing my gratitude to friends in academia and outside, too numerous to recount here, with whom I have over the years discussed the issues raised in this book, my immediate acknowledgment is due to the two referees who participated in the review process for this book and to Ian Malcolm, the editor, who combed through the whole manuscript suggesting many improvements and in general encouraged me throughout the publication process.

Index